Studies in Contemporary Indian Drama

Studies in
Contemporary Indian Drama

Edited by
SUDHAKAR PANDEY
FREYA TARAPOREWALA

PRESTIGE

PRESTIGE

Published by
Prestige Books
3/28, East Patel Nagar, New Delhi 110 008
in association with
Indian Society for Commonwealth Studies
New Delhi

1990

ISBN 81-85218-18-8

Jacket design by
3-A Corporation,
New Delhi 110 002

Phototypesetting by
data culture
New Delhi 110 065
Ph. 6431070

Printed at
Mehra Offset Press
New Delhi 110 002

Contents

Introduction 7

1. Contemporary Marathi Theatre
Dnyaneshwar Nadkarni 9

2. Experimental Marathi Theatre
Pushpa Bhave 16

3. Vijay Tendulkar: The Man Who Explores the Depths of Life
Chandrashekhar Barve 22

4. Protest as Art: Contemporary Hindi Drama
Aditya N. Agnihotri 26

5. *Shakuntal* and *King Lear* as studies in the King's Moral Orientation
Arun A. Bhagwat 32

6. He That Playeth the Sultan: A Study of *Tughlaq*
P. Ramamoorthi 38

7. The Development of Girish Karnad as a Dramatist: *Hayavadana*
Shubhangi S. Raykar 46

8. Experiment and Innovation in Modern Indian Drama in Translation: The Plays of Mohan Rakesh, Badal Sircar, Vijay Tendulkar and Girish Karnad
Veena Noble Dass 64

9. Domesticity and Drama: An Analysis of Nissim Ezekiel's *Marriage-Poem* and *Don't Call It Suicide*
Vrinda Nabar 75

10. Theme of Alienation in Nissim Ezekiel's Plays
R. Raj Rao 82

11. Panel Discussion on Gieve Patel's *Mister Behram* 92

Contributors 112

Introduction

This book is the compilation of papers and a panel discussion that were presented and held on the occasion of the first annual session of the **W.H. Golay Memorial Seminar,** organized by the Department of English, University of Poona. This is an annual seminar, held in the memory of W.H. Golay—a former Registrar, University of Poona—a keen admirer of theatre and drama, sponsored by Professor Leela Mulherkar, Director of the **W.H. Golay Memorial Fund.**

This Seminar took place on January 30 and 31, 1989, at the Department of English, University of Poona and included a performance on the evening of January 30, 1989, of Gieve Patel's new play **Mister Behram.**

This book contains three papers that were not presented at the Seminar due to exigencies of time. It is hoped that this book will contribute significantly to the study and appreciation of contemporary Indian drama.

The editors wish to express their gratitude to all those who contributed to the making of this book: Mrs A.A. Gayke, Mrs Jagtap and Mr Janardhan Nair for word-processing the manuscript; Mrs Toni Patel, for her painstaking transcription of the audio-taped recording of the panel discussion and especially Dr R.K. Dhawan for his constant help in arranging for the publication of this book.

Sudhakar Pandey
Freya Taraporewala
Editors

Contemporary Marathi Theatre

DNYANESHWAR NADKARNI

In 1943 the Marathi theatre celebrated its centenary in Bombay, Pune and Sangli. During the previous decade it had professionally fallen on evil days. The old glory of the Marathi musical theatre had disappeared long ago. The old company system was also disintegrating. Starting with the centenary celebrations, Dr. A.N. Bhalerao of the *Mumbai Marathi Sahitya Sangh* started organizing annual festivals of Marathi drama at open air theatres. The programme at these festivals consisted of revivals of established classics as well as performances of new plays. Well-known playwrights such as Anand Kanekar and V.V. Shirwadkar (this year's Jnanpith award-winner) started contributing adaptations as well as independently written plays to these festivals. Kanekar adapted from Glodsmith, Barrie and Galsworthy while Shirwadkar offered versions of Oscar Wilde, Maurice Maeterlinck and Shakespeare. Madhav Manohar was an even more prolific adapter, who used Maugham, Clifford Odets and Priestley for his work. It is against this enterprising background that we must see the growth of the contemporary Marathi theatre which began in the middle fifties.

Vijay Tendulkar leads the vanguard of the *avant-garde* theatre that developed as a movement separate from the mainstream. Tendulkar and his colleagues were dissatisfied not with the efforts of Dr. Bhalerao but with the decadent professional theatre that characterized the thirties and forties. They wanted to give theatre a new form and therefore experimented with all aspects of it including content, acting, decor and audience communication.

Tendulkar was a versatile writer of one-act plays. These plays of his use modern techniques of *avant-garde* in Europe and America. Tendulkar's full-length plays are comparatively conventional in format. These early full-length plays of his are a complete contrast to his later plays. They are full of an abiding humanity, genuine pathos and typical middle-class characters.

Shantata Court Chaloo Aahe comes as a turning point in Tendulkar's career. It has a play in rehearsal and a real-life story, and the two intertwine to produce some unusual dramatic confrontations. The plays *Gidhade, Sakharam Binder* and *Ghashiram Kotwal* may be considered a trilogy in the sense that they share a preoccupation with sex and the spirit of violence. *Gidhade* was probably intentionally written in order to prod the Marathi audience which, according to Tendulkar, had cultivated set ideas about what could and should be portrayed on the stage. *Sakharam Binder* is another shocker with its story of a womanizing low-class man having a flexible code of ethics.

Ghashiram Kotwal is an even more impressive achievement because it gives a totally new and self-contained form to the text. It is based on the historical conflict between Nana Phadnavis and his henchman Ghashiram Kotwal. There was much controversy over the authenticity of Nana as portrayed in this play. This can still go on but it is undeniable that this blend of spoken verse, varied music and highly original choreography directed by Jabbar Patel gave to the Marathi theatre an artistic experience worth cherishing for a long time.

Among Tendulkar's later plays few essay an experimental format worthy of his work of the middle period. Plays such as *Kamala* and *Kanyadan* are to be valued for their topicality, a quality inherent in Tendulkar's writing.

Vidyadhar Gokhale is often criticized for his lurid musical comedies, but two things must be remembered. First, that the type of the classical Marathi theatre was a special kind of musical play and second, that Vidyadhar Gokhale pioneered its revival in the sixties.

Gokhale's first play *Panditraj Jagannath* is not typical of the rest of his writing. He tries successfully to capture the spirit of the

Mughal era poet Jagannath Pandit who was as well versed in Urdu as in Sanskrit. His love-life, as portrayed here, travels on an idealized, imaginary plane, and on the whole the play hangs together and pleases in an intelligent way.

Gokhale's musical comedy *Suvarnatula* is modelled after Annasaheb Kirloskar's *Sangeet Saubhadra* which was first staged in 1982. One of the characters in both plays is the mischievous god Krishna. Both plays include Krishna's wife Rukmini. Gokhale's play for the first time has the rival wife Satyabhama and the comedy is about their rival demands on Krishna's love. The first production of the play was made memorable by the classically-oriented singing of old-timers like Chhota Gandharva.

Another musical play of Gokhale's to be considered as a genre product is *Mandarmala*. This can be compared with Kakasaheb Khadilkar's *Manapman* which the great Balgandharva had made a big hit in the early decades of this century. Both plays have an absurd and illogical plot rooted in an imaginary milieu. Both survive on the strength of their classically-oriented songs.

Gokhale has since written more plays but has long ago lost his impact. The Marathi musical theatre has once again fallen on bad days. The classics are badly produced, with atrocious costumes and decor although there are still singers of a high standard. But there are a few playwrights or artists who are setting new standards of creativity.

Jabbar Patel's productions of *Ghashiram Kotwal, Teen Paishacha Tamasha* and *Padgham* are exceptions to this rule but they are clearly products of the experimental theatre. *Teen Paishacha Tamasha* is a free-ranging version of Brecht's *Three-penny Opera* by P.L. Deshpande. It employs throughout tunes from rock or pop music. Their harnessing to Marathi songs is not entirely successful. *Padgham* is an independent play by the prolific novelist Arun Sadhu. It throws light on the current corruption within our body politic and within society. It employs a variety of music in an effective way.

On the whole, however, Marathi musical drama has reached a state of stagnation comparable to the decadence of early Marathi musical theatre which was co-terminous with the decline of Marathi drama before the Second World War.

Purushottam Laxman Deshpande stands as a solitary island in contemporary Marathi theatre. It is true that he has many adaptations and very few independently written plays to his credit, but his overall contribution to form in theatre is considerable. Also most of his adaptations are of significant Western plays.

P.L. started his career as a playwright by adapting Gogol's *The Government Inspector.* He himself acted the key role in the first production, and being adept at mimicry he could stamp that role with his own identity. After a few more adaptations, he came out in 1956 with *Tuze Aahe Tujapashi*, a unique satire in which an austere Gandhian Acharya fights a battle of ideas with an old epicure steeped in the ways of princely India. Three of P.L.'s plays have this background of a merged princely state.

At this time P.L. also started presenting his dramatic readings from his own Marathi humorous writings. The first, *Batatyachi Chawl,* presents the middle-class characters living in Batatyachi Chawl in the Girgaum area of Bombay. These specimens of bourgeoisie are ridiculed but at the same time their sense of values is praised. P.L. went on to offer more such one-man readings from his prolific humorous literature.

Where he created a new form was in the revue-oriented *Varyavarchi Varaat* and *Watwat Watwat.* These include sketches hilarious in their satirical wit and terms inspired by ruling Marathi folk/popular theatre forms. The whole amalgam had an exhilarating effect. P.L.'s own brand of humour has been common to these performances.

After *Teen Paishacha Tamasha,* P.L. translated *Raja Oidipous (Oedipus Rex)* from Sombhu Mitra's Bengali. It was never produced but given a reading by him at the time of the Emergency. One could hear strange echoes, in the situation in Thebes, as Sophocles described it, of the atmosphere of the Emergency.

P.L. Deshpande has recently given many poetry readings with his actress wife Sunita and also adapted a modern Soviet play. In P.L.'s work the mainstream and the experimental theatre merge without complaint.

In the experimental theatre the three major young playwrights who emerged after Tendulkar were Mahesh Elkunchwar, Achyut Waze and Satish Alekar. Of these, Waze has been inactive for a long time. Considering the innovative heights reached by him in a play like *Chalre Bhoplya Tunuk Tunuk,* his retirement from playwriting may be regretted. Elkunchwar started with some noteworthy one-act plays. They were made of solid substance and were sure of their experimental technique as well. He later wrote plays such as *Vasanakand, Garbo* and recently *Wada Chirebandi* and *Atmakatha.* Over the years he has gained in maturity and become essentially simpler in his plots and construction. *Wada Chirebandi* is conventional in technique. It portrays the breaking up of a joint family typical of the decadent landed gentry of Vidarbha. It has a set of unusual characters, both men and women. Atmakatha, in which Shriram Lagu inimitably acts the role of an old author, is even better. It employs many technical ploys with appropriate invention. The author's relationship with a girl student, with his wife and with his sister-in-law forms the dramatic matrix of this play.

Satish Alekar's best known play is *Mahanirvan.* It is a black comedy in the sense that it makes fun of the concept of death and uses the incident of a funeral to satirize blind conventions and religious orthodoxy. It alternates pathos with farcical comedy. Alekar's own production of the play is finely choreographed.

Ratnakar Matkari is a very prolific playwright who belongs as much to the experimental theatre as to the mainstream. Most notable among his plays is *Lokakatha '78*. This is based on a real life incident in rural Marathwada and uses experimental techniques. Each play of Matkari embodies fresh ideas and, even when it is not in an experimental format, is marked by depth and innovation.

Mainstream Marathi drama has a long tradition. Vasant Kanetkar is a senior playwright who started more than three decades ago with a dazzling experimental stance. However, as time passed by, only the structure has remained slightly unconventional. Kanetkar has long ago lost the innovative thrust of his first years.

Among at least dozen noteworthy plays by Kanetkar one

chooses *Raygadala Jevha Jaag Yete* and *Himalayachi Savli.* The first portrays the conflict between King Shivaji and his erring son Sambhaji on a human level. The second is based on the personality of the centenarian Dhondo Keshav Karve. The central roles in these plays were respectively played by Master Dattaram and Shriram Lagu, heroes of our finest thespians, the former a product of the classical theatre and the latter a protagonist of the *avant-garde.*

Like Kanetkar, V.V. Shirwadkar also belongs to the mainstream. This year's Jnanpith award-winner, he has written a series of tragedies and comedies that prove his genius. A few of his plays are based on historical or mythological heroes. He has ably adapted Shakespeare's *Macbeth* and *Othello* into Marathi. Shirwadkar's most outstanding play is *Natasamrat*, which carries clear echoes of *King Lear.* It is the harrowing tragedy of an old-time classical actor and is interspersed with Shakespearean soliloquies. Although a play of high quality, it has established instant communication with the mass audience simply because its theme is rooted in the popular theatre tradition of Maharashtra.

Bal Kolhatkar, the other senior mainstream playwright, is very sentimental and consistently plays to the gallery. He typifies a Marathi drama that has deteriorated owing to the needs of commercial exploitation. A majority of professional Marathi productions tour mofussil towns and they have compulsorily to appeal to the taste of the ordinary people that patronize them there. This is a problem and a challenge which eternally plagues some of the substandard playwrights.

The one playwright who has sustained hopes in the mainstream is Jaywant Dalvi. He has been prolific and fairly consistent. Among his early plays, *Sadhya-chhaya* and *Barrister* stand out as thematically substantial tragedies. The first portrays the plight of an old and lonely couple, while the second is the unusual tragedy of an England-returned barrister. Dalvi appears to focus quite a few of his plays on old couples. The latest in this class is *Kalchakra* which shows that the playwright's obsession has not adversely affected his quality. In the recent play *Sparsha*, Dalvi projects the peculiar dilemma of a family in which the mother is suspected of leprosy.

S.N. Navre started with a good experimental promise but the demands made by the commercial theatre on his prolix writing have completely sapped his quality. Thematically he has kept moving round and round in the same circle of family drama. He can be said to be a little better than Bal Kolhatkar, that purveyor of family melodrama, but his literary status is not high.

On the whole, mainstream drama in Marathi oscillates between authentic literary quality and the demands of business. Almost all Marathi drama companies are guided by the considerations of survival. Often they absorb or abduct playwrights and artistes from the *avant-garde*. But very naturally business comes first.

Among experimental playwrights G.P. Deshpande came out with a brilliant first in his *Udhavasta Dharmashala*. The protagonists of this play are a Marxist couple. The play is rooted in contemporary Maharashtrian politics and is unique for its telling contemporary references. It effectively dissects the socio-political situation that is around us and brings alive the characters thrown up by it. Deshpande, however, has not fulfilled his first promise.

The annual drama festival of the Maharashtra Government has over the years created an explosion of playwriting talent. Young playwrights such as P.L. Myakar have already come to stay and been welcomed by the mainstream. Plays such as *Shatakhanda* by Ajit Dalvi or *Jai Jai Raghuvir Samarth* by Premanand Gaji embody a hope for the future. There are quite a few other young playwrights who are writing in a promising experimental vein. Arun Naik's versions of *Macbeth* and *Othello* and Rajiv Naik's rendering of Shudraka's *Mrichhakatika* are extremely forward-looking experiments.

Marathi drama today can claim many young playwrights who have gone a step ahead of the generation of Tendulkar and Elkunchwar. They write with confidence and introduce formal novelties with admirable intelligence. On the whole, contemporary Marathi theatre presents a very hopeful picture, indeed.

Experimental Marathi Theatre

PUSHPA BHAVE

I will continue the theme of contemporary Marathi theatre begun by Mr. Nadkarni, emphasizing the work of the young playwrights: *Mahanirvan, Gochi, Chalre Bhoplya Tunuk Tunuk.* I do feel that *Mahanirvan* and *Chalre Bhoplya* have keyed in not to the Western Absurdist tradition, but created their own absurd language. I wrote this piece in answer to a question set at one of the American Centre seminars: Is the Absurd really relevant? Here the Absurd does not constitute amusement on the province of the futility of human endeavour. One meditates on the situation and arrives at a logic that makes this vision meaningless or trite. To project this style more effectively, dramatists have to forge a style more fluid, and more flexible than their predecessors. A generation, raised on the blare of radios and the dementia of railway platforms, can have no use for a theatre with a literary disposition using a slow unfolding of plot and character. Therefore it is not surprising that experiments in this area should have come from the pen and imagination of writers and directors operating in an urban milieu. The earliest evocation of this style came with *Gochi*, directed by Amol Palekar. Initially the play perplexed the audience, but it went on for nearly seventy-five performances. It is of considerable merit, when you take into account the nature of the content and the mode of presentation it involves. Gradually, the audience can regard it as an indigenous product—an offspring of urban youth. It is originally a Polish play translated into Marathi by Professor Sadanand Rege. The kind of sensibility presented in *Gochi* seemed applicable to our young—it is neither alien nor dissociated from our society. 'Gochi' was a word used in fourteenth or fifteenth century Marathi, which was beginning to get current again among the youth. Professor Rege picked up that word and used it anew. Rehearsing this play, the script changed with each rehearsal. As with Satyade Dube, the experimental director of Hindi drama, the actors and directors work intensively with the script, in evolving it. Similarly, *Gochi* seemed to conjure up a host of ideas or half-ideas and feelings. 'Gochi' could mean a problem, a crisis, a state of confusion, a bungling of sorts: the word soon acquired meaning in the modern urban context. The story involves Daddy, Mummy and brats. Daddy disappears and is reported missing. He finds himself near a site where two gravediggers are shovelling earth out of a ditch. (Notice the *Hamlet* theme, as in *Mahanirvan.*) When Daddy is traced, he refuses to return to his former self, because he can't. That is the bare skeleton of the performance. The play constantly trips to move to something beyond. At one level, Mummy tries desperately to recollect life with Daddy—she can only remember the brand of tea he likes and her efforts at recollecting the past only sink into clichés. In *Gochi,* there is this reduction of personality to trivia, to petty possessions. The two brats, commenting saucily on their parents are transformed into gravediggers. A quick flick of the hand and the style changes, when they assume the character of country folk using rough dialect. Such swift changes determine the pace. The play has never been performed in a proper auditorium—it is designed to take place anywhere—classrooms, courtyards, halls, without elaborate props. There are no entries or exits: when characters turn their back and move to a corner, they cease to exist. The dialogue, using nonsense words, i.e. 'kapa-mapa-rapa-thapa,' appears at moments when structured sentences may appear irrelevant; even the actors's expressions remain deadpan. Their bodies become subtle media of communication. The direction does not create a spectacle that is calculated to be pleasing to the eye. The music is more like the sound effects of tin-openers or wooden tools in action. This perplexed the older generation somewhat but managed to fascinate the young. They seemed to understand that the play was about their own lives, their own 'Gochi': with no storyline, no plot, no exits.

No one knew why Palekar caused Daddy to return with his head in his hands, but the audience realized that the gesture signified a lot.

The problem of what to do when confronted by the ultimate and then to return is the problem taken up also by the young dramatist Achyut Vaze in *Chalre Bhoplya Tunuk Tunuk*. The title is from a Marathi nursery rhyme. Audiences were scared out of their wits, when they went expecting children's theatre and discovered an avant-garde play. It centres around an ordinary domestic situation. Wandrekar arrives to occupy a room in Bhausaheb's house. Mentally, he hugs his 'Bhoplya,' his pumpkin. The huge round pumpkin with its mincing jerky walk can mean any number of things: it may be the job he's looking for, or the feeling of love for his landlord's daughter or the hope centred in marriage or in expectations surrounding his unborn child. The hymn to the pumpkin, which at the beginning sounded so trite and funny, now sounds dead-serious and frightening at times.

Another play, originating from Pune this time, communicated the same sensibility, but operated on different lines: this is *Mahanirvan*. I feel that Satish Alekar has often been accused of being out of tradition. I feel that he is entrenched in tradition, but uses it in a different way as in the use of Sane Guruji, the freedom movement and middle-class morality. He has developed his own style of the Absurd, with relevant links with the tradition. A middle-class chawl-dweller dies—a situation which seems initially, to be similar to plays from an earlier period, but which in this play, is treated in a manner entirely different. Before *Mahanirvan*, we had a series of plays about the middle-class, such as P.L. Deshpande's *Batatechi Chawl*. Though Deshpande's sphere was a coherent intelligible habitat, with ordinary people with faults and idiosyncracies, yet a warm homely universe, unlike that of *Mahanirvan*. Death never made its appearance there. In *Mahanirvan*, a particular individual's death becomes the starting point for an examination of life. The neighbours bustle around the corpse. The atmosphere is redolent of the self-importance and finesse that accompanies our funeral rites. The situation is brilliantly realized in song and dance. Nana, the son, is away attending a sports tourney when his father dies. The way the neighbours break the news to him when he returns is tinged with hilarity. Since the sports tourney is at the back of their mind, they assume the positions of the game he has just played: "atya-patya" they take their positions on the stage. The dead man is the narrator: he does not say his lines in straightforward pose, but recites them in the kirtan style. He is carried to the burning grounds. They discover that a new municipal regulation has come into force—the grounds have been closed down. However, the dead man nurses an attachment to the place and will not allow his body to be burnt anywhere else. Young Nana has on his hands the foul, decaying body of his father and his all-pervasive presence. This is a very complete play. On the one hand, the *Hamlet* symbol, on the other, the father-son relationship. The widowed mother is representative of the disintegrating personality. She contemplates the empty frame created by the loss of her husband. This is filled by the obsessive memory of a faceless male wearing a suit and dark glasses. Who is he? How is Nana to discover the identity of this individual and solve the mystery? Nana bribes the sentries and arranges illegally for the funeral. The dead man sings and dances with joy as the flames consume him. Nana looks forward to his own future—the possibilities of his own sexual desires being satisfied. *Mahanirvan* is physically a representation of our middle-class life-style in its present anachronistic context. The usual round of rice is brought for crows to peck at, after the funeral, but it is a pitiful amount in the kind of box in which clerks carry their lunch. The details are meticulously set out, but in a way that ceases to provoke or shock, but mirrors the facts of life. A play centering around a corpse could easily degenerate into necrophilia, but the playwright deftly avoids morbidity or hysteria. The corpse comments upon its own predicament in dance and song. The chawl-dwellers revel in their role as counsellers to the son and find release in dance.

In the midst of this lively presentation, what the spectators are made to realize is that this play is about death and life: the rhythms and realizations cannot be effaced. Of course, objections have been raised against this theatre style. The critics who like to designate theatre styles have labelled such plays, Indian versions of western black comedy. None of these artists has claimed that, but since they come from metropolitan backgrounds like their Western counterparts, they react in similar or identical forms. Even so, their style or artistic form is such that it could only have emerged from the Western strip of Maharashtra. Another school of criticism upbraids this style for its lack of social relevance and considers these works a waste of talent and time. In a sense, these young people are more committed to social and political change than their critics, but they are honest enough in not seeking their solutions in political or social remedies, and intelligent enough not to allow their inventiveness to be put down by the weight of their dogma.

If and when they embark on the Theatre of Protest, they are now well on the way, due to plays like *Juloos* or *Party* by Elkunchwar. There are others who exhort these young playwrights to turn to the rich folk traditions of our land. Their answer to this is that they are not in search of exotica and that they are not moved by a nostalgia for the past that is irrevocably lost, of a strong folk tradition germane to a community of people knit together by ties of strong feeling. Their drama refers to a society where a man is seized with fright at communicating with a fellow being in his innermost self. If the folk means anything to them, it is a vague terrain, a tug at the memory. In *Mahanirvan,* the kirtan emerging from the lips of a rotting corpse loses all piety. The only possible response to this form in frantic and empty lives is one that almost verges on parody. That is why these playwrights refuse to embark on a journey of discovery, digging up their roots in a remote past. They want to be rooted, if at all, in the reality of their own existence and when they do move away from their immediate surroundings into another area, it is not one of make-believe. True enough, it is akin to fantasy, as absurd and bizarre as the texture of life. A stray word sometimes unleashes a barrage of associations and the actors sometimes break into incantations, and spells. This is different from the method of Badal Sircar, a Bengali playwright of the previous generation. He carefully structures a play around the loss of identity or rejection of spontaneous love. But his characters analyze their predicament in coherent phrases or terms. Our absurdist actors, however, act it out with their deadpan frozen facial expressions, the machine-like movements of their bodies while presenting their outer and inner lives. So these theatre events relate to a climate, a state of mind. They define experiences that are incarnated in the here and now, yet inherently related to neither of these. Glued to the trivialities of existence, they reveal in the performance, a yearning that is vague and near-abstract. They accept the world around them on its own terms. Their main characters are not exceptional beings, but non-heroes like themselves. Their thoughts are so knotted up by their routinized present, yet each one among them would cry out for something larger and freer. Whether the style has exhausted its possibilities, the next few years will decide. Right now, when one considers these artists and their work, one recalls their pluck, their nerve, backed with their sheer talent laced with the sort of intensity and irony that made theatre-going these last three years more than worthwhile.

Extract from the recorded transcription of Mrs. Bhave's oral presentation.

Vijay Tendulkar:
The Man Who Explores the Depths of Life

CHANDRASHEKHAR BARVE

Vijay Tendulkar is the most turbulent and controversial dramatist among the modern Marathi playwrights. His plays *Sakharam Binder, Ghashiram Kotwal* created a storm in society and at the same time he won the highest award in the field of dramatics, on an all-India level, for his play *Shantata, Court Chaloo Aahe.* No wonder his literary personality has proved to be very interesting by inviting hate and high honour simultaneously.

The understanding of Tendulkar the dramatist can never be complete without considering the background of his extra-dramatic writing; a precise evaluation of his work is still more difficult. His literary tendency can be observed through his numerous articles, middles, short-stories and one-act plays. He can rejoice in the beauty and nobility in the world but he is not blind to the ugly and ignoble in it. Though his eyes are focused on the middle-class and its suffocations, his chief targets are the human mind, the way of life and the complexities therein. While depicting the man-woman relationship, he shows something uncommon and strange; but it is equally true that he never gives a perverted and vulgar form to this depiction. Tendulkar's articles, stories and one-act plays reveal that his literary tendency is of realistic, soft but poignant expression.

The outline of Tendulkar's dramatic taste is evident from his articles on drama, his reviews of plays and films, appreciation of dramatic monologues in prose (Natya-chhata), the translated plays, children's plays and some of his noble one-act plays. He does not crave for outdated ideals or impossible aims. He is drawn towards "the real," with all its limitations. Human existence, the deep understanding of human psychology and expressing them through drama is an obsession with him. He prefers restraint and simplicity to excessive freedom and gaudiness. He seems to like the serious and tragical plays more—the plays which show the essential nature of man—the exposed, penetrating plays. His extra-dramatic writing also reveals his pure taste for drama which tries to capture the different tensions and through them, finds "the dramatics" accurately.

His dramatic creations from *Shreemant* to *Pahije Jateeche* are no exceptions to this rule. Right from the beginning upto this date, Tendulkar is drawn towards the basic and eternal conflict in human life—the conflict between two strong desires to live where ultimately even one's blood-relations prove false and brittle. While developing this conflict he uses the satirical, sharp and biting style. He traces the roots of this conflict to the social, domestic and psychological levels. However, he does not expose them directly in the play. Tendulkar mostly exhibits men trying to live independently as human beings drifting along the current of the inevitable, like a lifeless, capsized boat, in his characteristic cool manner.

The depiction of life in Tendulkar's plays has an invisible but solid foundation in his philosophy of life. His philosophy of life includes Man, his body and soul, his ego, his associations, the futility in the relations between men, the resultant sense of loneliness, the ideas of sin and virtue, the uncertainty of all these; in short the individual identity of man and his social existence, the harmony and disharmony between the two—these form the essence of Tendulkar's thinking. Tendulkar's plays don't appear to carry the burden of intellectual speculation. And yet (perhaps because of this very reason), they remain beyond the shallow, hollow and the cheap, telling us silently, something original, beyond words. Considering all this, it can be observed that Tendulkar's plays tend towards existentialism.

The psychological conflicts in the play *Madhlya Bhinti* are the result of excessive self-love. Parwatibai is dejected because her wish is ignored; while Sadashiv is sad because someone else's desire has been imposed on him. This means, both the characters intensely desire that their *egos* should manifest themselves freely and strongly. When this becomes impossible, they are terribly annoyed. We can conclude that *Madhlya Bhinti* is a play about the manifestation, assertion and superiority of the egos and about the conflicts about them. Sadashiv says, "Finally there is just one relation—relation to the self." These words of Sadashiv are indicative of the central substance of the play.

The existentialist tendencies in Tendulkar are anticipated in *Madhlya Bhinti* while they are clearly discernible in *Shantata Court Chaloo Aahe.* This is not a play about the cornering of Benare, nor about the cornered Benare. In fact the dramatic element in it is derived from the situation in which the "being" of Benare is engulfed by the social existence of her individuality. She tries to express her ego openly and freely; and finally it is throttled. "Life is something like nothingness"—these crazy words of Benare are good comment on the nothingness of our "being."

These existentialist tendencies are openly manifest in *Sakharam Binder.* Sakharam's ego tries to manifest itself in a challenging way. It is not ready to be tied down to anything. The influence of Laxmi triggers an inner conflict in Sakharam—the conflict between the existential ego and the metaphysical I. In effect we see that Sakharam, who has lost his self, has become pitiable because of his spinelessness, very much like a string without a kite. When he realizes that he is losing himself, he goes astray, he is frightened and finally his living corpse gets pacified after lifeless and senseless activities. Sakharam is unpolished and hence the play *Sakharam Binder* appears to be rough. Nevertheless, the play does make its appearance with existentialist traits. To sum up, Tendulkar was the pioneer who changed not only the external framework of Marathi drama but also the limits of the picture of life at the core.

Tendulkar's plays helped to refine Marathi drama that was so far polluted by propaganda for political awakening, and social reforms, cheap and vulgar entertainment. The only reason for this being that he began writing plays after delving deep into human relations. He did not indulge in painting superficial conflicts in gaudy colours, on the other hand he painted the egotistic tensions, effectively in pastel shades. No other Marathi dramatist seems to have done this before. Since 1955, he has written over twenty plays. He deserves credit; for he not only gave a pure dramatic taste to the Marathi play, but also cultivated that taste to focus it on the very existence of one's "being," directing it to the origin, to the subtle.

Today, we cannot say it with certainty that Tendulkar will be a celebrity of the Marathi drama scene. However, we can say this with certainty that Tendulkar has guided Marathi drama that seemed to have lost its proper track, and has kept leading it for over two decades. His place and importance in this respect shall remain unique in the history of Marathi drama. There may be controversies regarding his greatness but his achievements are beyond question. There isn't any doubt about this, there shouldn't be any.

Somewhere, Tendulkar has said, "I have drifted to the middle of the current of life. I now feel its unfathomable depths. Like the sea-birds, I am soaring aimlessly, casually and calmly . . . I have only one desire--How deep would be the bottom? How would it appear?" Whatever he saw, Tendulkar has portrayed in his plays. Let him see more of it in the days to come. Let him portray it in his future plays.

Translated by:

Prof. Ajit Soman
Prof. Arun Belsare

Protest as Art: Contemporary Hindi Drama

ADITYA N. AGNIHOTRI

Prior to initiating a provocative discussion such as "Protest as Art: Contemporary Hindi Drama," I had better define and delimit the parameters of my paper. Broadly speaking, every work of art in its final analysis turns out to be a protest of sorts, implied or implicit. This perhaps is the underlying notion of the dictum: "All art is protest." The word "Protest" in the present context has been used with a different connotation, however. Protest here means a deliberate, conscious expression of disgust at and disapproval of situations, the horrid web of tensions and dilemmas the common man finds himself in. It analyzes, exposes, agitates against and assaults the system responsible for man's present day plight and suffering. Protest as such has immense artistic potential.

Protest as art, like any other art, delights; it delights by not only convincingly exposing the system under study, it delights by satisfying one's sense of disgust and anger against that system by effectively voicing the inarticulate urges of the common man, and it delights by satisfying one's sense of beauty by consciously or unconsciously conveying the artist's own vision of it, his own concept of a beautiful life as also of idealized human behaviour clearly or implicitly stated. Thus, protest as art projects a multiple experience, agitating, energizing, ennobling and yet delighting all at the same time.

When an artist finds life miserably wanting in things that make it worth-living, his sense of beauty (which is also his sense of justice as also of moral and spiritual values) is enraged and he protests. His immediate reaction is to demolish the system responsible for the hellish state of affairs. And unlike a professional politician or a social scientist, or a crime reporter or a statistician engaged in a socio-economic survey, his restless spirit will not rest content with the mere 'exposition' of it. He will no doubt expose the establishment to register his protest against it, to share with his readers/ audience his deep sense of disgust against it, but he will not stop there. He will 'agitate' against it, he will agitate the minds of those who share his sentiments. This 'agitation' is the end-product of protest as art and is often responsible for many a social and political revolution in the history of human civilization.

The 'agitation' caused by the artist's protest is a compound of several discernible ingredients: shock, anger, identity of purpose, and an inner compulsion to strive for the realization of a vision propounded or just suggested by the artist through his protest wherein the ugliness of 'what is' is thrown into relief by contrasting it with the beauty of 'what should be.' Social protest in art at least is an outline of an utopia.

When an artist confronts a situation he cannot appreciate, much less tolerate, he protests and his protest takes a variety of forms depending on his perception, intensity of feeling, intellectual awareness, vision, his imaginative experience and capacity to 'sense' things; in short, his artistic sensibility and finesse, and most important of all, his purpose.

Obviously, the protest may be either (a) personal, that is, intensely subjective and self-centred or (b) social, that is, intensely philanthropic and full of concern for the welfare of all.

Broadly speaking, these forms may also be conditioned by (a) socio-cultural ethos of the people involved, (b) by the author's sense of history, (c) by his own vision and (d) by audience-anticipation, and the forms of protest may be broadly classified accordingly.

Protest in Tulsidasa's *Ramcharitmanas* with his vision of Ramraj belongs to the visionary class. Protest conditioned, or rather inspired, by the author's anticipation of the audience interest is, like all instant literature, topical, racy even spicy but with hardly any claims to commend itself to posterity. There is more of pamphleteering in it than of durable human concern.

What is usually termed as 'protest' in art is in fact an unromantic realization of social imbalances where the artist's sympathies gang up on the side of the deprived. This sympathy may be purely commisserative in which case the artistic response gets sentimental or it may be a historical realization in which case the artistic response becomes Marxist or it may be an objective assessment of the contemporary social situation in which case the artist is said to be writing in the tradition of realism.

Before dealing with contemporary Hindi drama with protest as its focal point I should like to give a hurried resume of the history of Hindi Drama. Hindi Drama begins with the satirical and realistic comedies of Bhartendu Harish Chandra: *Bharat Durdashe, Andher Nagri* and *Vaidiki Hinse Na Bhavati.* It was the beginning of a new awareness of the reality of the Indian situation. However, it could not be expanded to fullness for lack of competent followers. Barring an exception or two like Radhacharan Goswami and Pratap Narain Mishra who satirized social conditions obtaining in rural India, there is a clear gap of several decades in Hindi play-writing. In fact, the genuine beginning of Hindi play-writing is made with the advent of Jai Shankar Prasad's historical plays: *Kamana, Vishakha, Ajatashatru, Janmejaya Ka Nagayagya, Skandagupta, Chandragupta* and *Dhruvaswamini.* These plays though mostly historical and rooted in Indian culture are a conscious effort at revitalizing Indian nationalism by contrasting the colonial degradation of India with a romantic visualization of the glorious past of the country. "Prasad's plays stand midway between the romantic poetic drama and the realistic problem play." (Ram Vilas Sharma, Hindi Drama, *Indian Literature,* New Delhi, vol. I, no. 2, 1958, p. 92).

"After Prasad," Dr. Sharma further observes, "Hindi drama came nearer to realism through mythical and historical themes." Udai Shankar Bhatt, Hari Krishna 'Premi,' Govind Ballabh Pant, Govind Das Seth, Ram Kumar Verma, Vishnu Prabhakar and Upendra Nath 'Ashk' figure prominently during this period. Premi's *Rakhi Ki Laj* deals with the problem of communalism, Ashk's *Chhota Beta* and Prabhakar's *Doctor* deal with family crisis.

The dramatic technique and structure undergo a sea-change after Prasad. Lakshmi Narain Mishra's plays *Sanyasi: Mukti Ka Rahasya* and *Sindoor Ki Holi* espouse the cause of individual liberty against religious and socio-religious regimentation. Dharma Veer Bharati's *Andha Yug* presents the tragic conflict of values. So does Dushyant Kumar's *Ek Kantha Vispayie* dealing with horrors of war, which is also a protest against repression and exploitation. Mohan Rakesh's *Ashad Ka Ek Din* and *Laharon Ke Rajhans* deal with the man-woman relationship. His *Aadhe Adhoore* reflects the crisis of the family tensions of middle-class people.

Lakshmi Narain Lal, Mudra Rakshas, and Rakesh Bakshi protest and revolt against the establishment. Their treatment is fiercely farcical in most cases, even absurdist and existentialist. Lal's *Abdulla Diwana,* Mudra Rakshas's *Marjeeva,* Surendra Verma's *Draupadi* and Bhisham Sahni's *Hanus* are fine examples of this species of play-writing. Of particular interest is Mudra Rakshas's burlesque adaptation (in Nautanki Form) of Gogol's *Inspector General* as *Aala Afsar.*

Protest through re-interpretation of mythological themes and legends, their re-employment or rather purposive adaptation to expose and assault the horrid contradictions and hypocrisy of our modern set up is a remarkable phenomenon in contemporary Hindi drama. Shankar Shesh's *Ek Aur Dronacharya* and *Raktabeej,* Daya Prakash Sinha's *Katha Ek Kans Ki,* Lal's *Mr. Abhimanyu* and *Suno Janmejay,* Ramesh Bakshi's *Devayani Ka Kahana Hai* and Ramesh Gaur's *Ek Aur Chakravyuha* use mythology with masterly finesse with an effect that is simply terrific.

Our present-day socio-political as also religio-cultural system with its obvious contradictions, hypocrisies, corruption, atrocities and its ostrich-like denials of the same, the hollowness of its claims and promises and its sham concern for values provide a vast and varied harvest of themes to write on. And never before were symbols, satire and irony employed with such deadly, devastating effect as witnessed today, Sarveshwar's *Bakari,* Sharad Joshi's *Andhon Ka Hathee* and *Ek Gadha,* Kusum Kumar's *Sanskar Ko*

Namaskar, Nag Bodos's *Kriti Vikriti,* Surrendra Tiwari's *Ek Tha Raja,* Pratap Sehgal's *Rang Basanti,* Rameshwar Premi's *Charpayee,* Giriraj Kishore's *Praja Hi Rahane Do,* Gyandeo Agnihotri's *Shuturmurga,* Sushil Kumar Singh's *Sinhasan Khali Hai,* Mrinal Pandey's *Jo Rachi Rakha,* Ishgar Veghat's *Enna Ki Awaz,* Dhirendra Asthana's *Arambha,* Ishaque Siddique's *Kutte* and Aditya Agnihotri's *Mataka* are some of the examples of the vitriolic assault on the system through satire and irony and symbols that are intensely pungent and purposive.

Protest in contemporary Hindi Drama is mostly in the nature of situations underlined. The playwright confronts reality against the value system he espouses and in the context of the horrid web of tensions woven by developments in modern life. He challenges the validity and relevance of tradition and old values, he exposes the ugliness of a system that dehumanizes and tramples on human dignity and he refrains from imposing a solution, as such an effort invariably tends to dilute the protest and its artistic appeal. Happily such instances (of imposing a solution) are rare in contemporary Hindi Drama.

Hindi Drama today, as Narendra Mohan in his *The Eternal 'No': Dimensions of Protest in Hindi Literature* rightly observes, is "protest oriented." It is intensely critical of a system that deshapes man and exposes the dilemma of modern life at various levels. The Hindi playwright today is communicating this protest with an awareness and purposive intensity hitherto unknown in Hindi drama of yesteryears thanks to the shaping influence of western drama as also of Marathi, Bengali, Gujarati, Tamil and Kannada drama.

A word about the Hindi stage and its idiom. Contemporary Hindi drama has witnessed giant strides in stagecraft, dramatic idiom and structure during the past two decades. The conventional stage (inherited from Parsi theatrical companies) with its painted curtains depicting forts, palaces, city streets, cluster of cottages, seas, rivers, mountains and forests etc. was replaced by the one or two-set stage which is further simplified by a suggestive set or no-set stage. Five acts yielded place to one act, the emphasis being on compactness rather than expansion. Technically, the entire emphasis of Hindi drama today is on suggestive or symbolic characters and make-up, credible costumes and acting. The speech of contemporary Hindi drama has also undergone a sea-change. It is more convincing, evocative, nearer to the common man's idiom. The difference of Hindi and Urdu is fast disappearing, at least the artificial line of demarcation and the writers's obsessive concern with the so-called purity of speech are no more there.

Of late we are witnessing a unique phenomenon: the rise of people's theatre—the theatre of resistance and mass motivation. Of all the art-forms protest finds its most vocal, most powerful and effective expression in drama. It has the unmatched advantage of live contact with the people it purports to reach and move. However, the growing impatience and aggressiveness that we witness today in the wayside plays, or *Nukkad Nataks,* Safdar Hashmi's *Halla Bol* for instance, is not entirely free from hazards. From the confines of the theatre hall, drama has now come out in the open, at the crossroads. Where it shall go from here can be anybody's guess. The propagandist stance with its political vocabulary, with its usual jargon materialistic Marxist-interpretation of history, class-consciousness, class-war, mass action etc. may lead to aberrations verging on pamphleteering thus risking its excellence as an art form. What the future holds in store for contemporary Hindi drama I dare not predict. But of one thing I feel fairly certain: protest as the focal point of contemporary Hindi drama is still on the rise and in spite of its occasional partisan outbursts it may produce a classic or two of its own in the not too distant future.

Shankuntal and *King Lear* as Studies in the King's Moral Orientation

ARUN A. BHAGWAT

Kalidasa's *Abhignyanashakuntala* and Shakespeare's *King Lear* are commonly regarded as the finest and most comprehensive expressions, not only of the respective artists's mature dramatic vision but as master-statements of the ethos in which each was written. Moreover, the works can be approached as two of the core texts which can lead to a better comparative understanding of the east and west. It may be noted that Rabindranath Tagore attempted a comparative study—which of course includes an equally careful consideration of differences—of Shakespeare and Kalidasa in *Pra-china Sahitya.* He was probably the first critic to compare and contrast Shakuntala and Miranda.

I have tried here in a somewhat cursory manner to explore the possibility of looking at the great classics in a comparative light. I believe that in spite of the obvious differences in structure, style and vision, each work revolves round a similar ethical concern, namely the king's error of judgement, which springs from his perceptual problem. Each of the kings—Dushyanta and Lear—repudiates the female which plays a central role in his life. Ironically, the king, while rejecting the female, thinks that he is acting in the name of justice. He persists in this error of judgement when there is reason to pause and reflect. Shortly after the rejection he realizes that he has cast not only himself, but his kingdom, into the hands of blind fate. He must suffer as a consequence of his rejection of divine grace itself. In the rough course of his later life he is fortunate enough to be reunited with his beloved daughter and attain her forgiveness.

Also, both the works highlight the king as a representative of mankind—not as a power symbol but as a sufferer. His fall from grace is the result of his unique predicament: his royal status is, of necessity, fostered by the conventions and rituals of monarchy. Each of them is a successful ruler—perhaps too successful. Partly through his own deserts and partly through the ceremonies of the royal court he has come to view himself as larger than life. This is surely unfortunate because many of his choices are governed by his private self—the passion and appetites the flesh is heir to. There is a continuity between man and king. This divine-human paradox is the chief cause of his error and suffering. Through the suffering the God-man paradox is grasped and transcended.

From one viewpoint, it strikes me that no two writers could have lived in such dissimilar times. Shakespeare's Renaissance was an age of storm and stress. We see here the co-presence of mutually opposed forces like excitement about the vast human potential and anxiety about the chaotic and destructive possibilities in blind human ambition. The orthodox Christian faith, comfortably embedded in the Ptolemaic world-view was now unable to comfort the young intellectual. On the other hand the new knowledge, British commercial ventures and the Machiavellian political models could easily induce ruthless self-seeking coupled with a cynicism about the time-honoured socio-political institutions. In short, the age of individualism had arrived and everything that happened seemed to foster and consolidate it.

Kalidasa's age, on the other hand, is firmly rooted in the past. There is no anxiety or scepticism whatsoever. The great confrontation between Hinduism on the one hand and Buddhism and Jainism on the other had already begun and so had the 'internationalization' of India in the sense of the commercial contact with China and Rome. But Vedic Hinduism was unruffled and the Hindu artist went about his creation in the spirit of tranquillity—especially the artist upon whom the royal court had smiled. Unlike the western Renaissance artist who saw man challenged by the combined forces of inner and outer disorder, the Indian artist saw human life as the triple assemblage of *satva, raja* and *tama* (the psycho-ethical categories which can be roughly translated as the self-effacing, self-oriented and selfish) in which each individual worked out his own salvation according to his dharma. Order pervaded both the micro and the macrocosm. If an individual behaved chaotically, it was through his own ignorance. Its removal automatically restored him to this order.

However, there is an important concern which seems to be common to Kalidasa as well as Shakespeare—namely, the integrity of the king and the welfare of the state. Shakespeare's Histories share this theme with his Great Tragedies; Kalidasa's *Raghuvansha* a 'historical epic' is a study of excellence in kings. 'Honour' is an important leitmotif in Shakespeare whereas the concept of Rajadharma is almost an equivalent term in Kalidasa. There is a difference of approach. Shakespeare, the realist, saw the divine right theory in an ambivalent perspective: Divine justice illustrating itself in the political affairs of the state is often such a subjective notion that almost anyone contending for power can evoke it. As legitimate heirs, usurpers and manipulators rise and fall, the historical patterns illustrate the paradox of human fallibility coexistent with royal divinity. Very few kings approximate to the concept of ideal kingship; whereas Kalidasa the idealist chooses to celebrate kings who are partly historical and partly mythological, for in the contemporary Indian notion of history fact merged with fiction, the mundane with the supernatural. His kings can be broadly divided into warriors, ascetics and men of pleasure and often in his ideal kings the three traits integrate. Pleasure and soldierly impulses surface at the appropriate moments and asceticism comes as the culmination of an eventful life. All the kings portrayed before Dushyanta are basically simple types on the lines of *satva* and *raja* or in keeping with the aesthetic categories of *dheera-lalita-uddatta* or *udhdhata*, i.e. the various combinations of the playful, noble, brave and heroic.

It is in *Shakuntal* that Kalidasa creates a king whose portrayal shows a degree of complexity. A typical pleasure-seeker of the *Kamasutra*, an acute observer of nature and human nature, an efficient administrator and magistrate, a poet and a fierce soldier (the last portrayed in supernatural colours—the side of Indra), Dushyanta is all these rolled into one. He is Kalidasa's version of Everyman. He has his human weaknesses and they spring directly from the most exacting tasks that his kingship demands. He, like the sun-god, knows no rest, for the welfare of the earth depends upon them both, possibly his pleasure trips, like the royal hunting expeditions, serve a double purpose of keeping himself and his army in shape and reminding his subjects of his might. His love-life consists of keeping many women happy by impressing on each (without the knowledge of the others) that he loves her exclusively. His life is full of game-playing. And each game is a special device to keep him fighting-fit as the head of the state. He has specific advisors in the complex matters of *dharma, artha* and *kama*. But he often craves of the unaffected, spontaneous modes of life and hence his impulsive and over-powering infatuation for Shakuntala. He must win her at once. So long as he does not know her heart he spends sleepless nights and once he is sure of her favours he does not wait for Kanva's consent. Dushyanta is basically noble but he is impulsive like an adolescent. Even without the curse of Durvasa and the ring which plays havoc in their life, the Dushyanta-Shakuntala relationship is fraught with fatal possibilities—Hansapadika's love-lorn song mildly accusing Dushyanta of inconstancy points to a similar future state of Shakuntala as a possibility. Dushyanta is deeply wounded by the beauty of Hansapadika's song but he is untouched by the suffering behind the beauty. Memories of some past existence stir uneasily in him but the immediate sorrow of Hansapadika is lightly dismissed as a playful taunt. Delicate irony constantly interacts with genuine artistic sympathy making Dushyanta the most original royal character in Kalidasa's works.

Without elaborating further I would like to conclude that Kalidasa is consciously and subtly subverting the time-honoured dramatic convention of the noble *(udatta)* hero, in order to convey the conflict as it would have taken place in a real-life situation between a passionate but well-meaning king and an artless maid. The source story in the *Mahabharata* gives us a different kind of confrontation in a very crude way. There the conflict is between a cunning king and a possessive girl who is anything but naive. Kalidasa in his infinitely more refined version presents the story as a divine comedy, the progress of a soul through error and suffering to self-realization; but an uncritical assumption that the ring and curse episodes are the poet's devices to absolve the hero of blame does grave injustice to Kalidasa's imaginative handling of the material by oversimplifying the play's message.

Kalidasa tells the story of a king who is in the final analysis a man in flesh-and-blood in his worship of the senses and his yearning for genuine love. These impulses are often at loggerheads and unless properly integrated, tend to degenerate into utter selfishness. Shakespeare takes a very old king who is far more self-assured than Dushyanta of the essential nobility of his desires. The latter's comfortable assertion that Shakuntala must be the proper match for him *because* his noble heart is yearning for her has a touch of childlike elation: Lear's act of taking Cordelia's obedience for granted is terrifying and her refusal to pamper this complacency followed by his savage wrath ending in Cordelia's rejection make the second scene of *King Lear* (Act I) almost unparalleled even in Shakespeare, as a source of energy needed to move the artifice of such magnitude. Another soul has begun a far more terrifying journey which will give him so little at the cost of so much—a few moments of happiness with Cordelia preceded and succeeded by agonies that unhinge him. Lear cries in agony that he is 'a man more sinned against than sinning.' The universe is indifferent; the winter storm rages on, mad Tom utters incoherences which mean and don't mean much to Lear. Kent cannot reveal his identity and Gloucester is blind. The fool adds to his agony unknowingly. Cordelia alone can bring real solace but finally he has to witness even this solitary tie snap. His final question 'why should a cat, a dog, have life and there no breath at all?' is not a rhetorical question. The heavens are probably empty and there is no answer. His final words, 'Look at her lips' possibly mean that they are moving and so she is not dead. He dies with some relief that she is alive.

Shakuntal and *King Lear* are possibly the finest instances of two most significant modes in world literature: the divine comedy and tragedy, respectively. The former aims at a comprehensiveness. The whole truth about human life has to be told. The message can come through only if the artist and the audience share certain common assumptions about the nature, scope and goals of human life, if not a common religion. Intellectual doubt, which alienates man from the universe as well as from himself is extraneous to the divine comedy and so is the sorrow it generates. It is far less esoteric than tragedy. It makes modest claims on the reader's stamina. Its paradigm is the act of worship in which every ritual must lead further along the way of meditation and every factor contributing to any strain should be carefully eliminated. Lucidity of perception is the integral component of its enjoyment.

Tragedy, on the other hand, is a form of Hatha Yoga, an elaborate process of self-discipline consisting of endurance tests. As the psyche suffers it craves for more—not in a perverse, masochistic manner but in a positive way, to increase one's capacity to stand more and more of reality. When one's alienation from the inner and outer world is complete and one can accept the naked, forked animal within, one can feel and even relish the peace after the battle.

The divine comedy binds people together and celebrates the sense of belonging. Tragedy celebrates something else—man's uniqueness of perception in spite of his vulnerability to the forces of destruction within and without.

He That Playeth the Sultan: A Study of *TUGHLAQ*

P. RAMAMOORTHI

Girish Karnad's *Tughlaq* deserves a close scrutiny as it highlights one of the fundamental concepts of theatre i.e. that theatre is an illusion, a fleeting shadow, a vision and a dream-like experience. There is a close parallel between life and theatre and quite often life is theatre-like and vice versa. But at no time life is theatre and theatre is life. The thin line of demarcation between good theatre and life is very often not perceived and hence the confusion and misunderstanding that both are the same or both are interchangeable. A skilful playwright, even when he is realistic, makes us conscious: Look here! You're only watching a *play*. There are several ways of bringing in this awareness into the audience. A dramatist may, like Brecht, use epic distancing or use "fantasy" as Gene does, or he might use certain images to suggest that the audience is undergoing a theatrical experience. Girish Karnad uses theatrical images in *Tughlaq* to achieve an effect that is comparable to the achievement of John Osborne in *Luther*.

There are many references to acting, theatre, and performance in *Tughlaq*. Muhammad behaves and speaks like an actor. His public appearance and his private moments are like that of an actor. In the opening scene itself there is a reference to his theatricality. He appears before the crowd properly heralded, and waxes eloquent. He speaks of "justice," "peace," "purposeful life"—rather he uses cliches to describe his desires. He makes an "exhibition" of his sense of justice. When he leaves the scene, the Guard disperses the crowd shouting at them:

> All right, all right. Go home! What are you waiting for? The *show's over!* Go home. . . .[1] (Italics mine) (5)

The Sultan's public appearance, his sense of justice, his plans are all a part of the show. The crowd is the audience for the Sultan. It looks more or less like a scene from the street-theatre. Even after the actors have moved into another part of the city the audience sometimes lingers on and comments on the players and their performance. The Guard's appraisal of the situation is clear and incisive. Just as the Guard judges the situation, in Scene Two, the stepmother sees Sultan as an actor. She laughs at his performance and that is a positive sign of the acting potentiality of the Sultan as an actor. She asks a simple question: "Then what do you do all night?" (10) and the reply is a lengthy, *theatrical* monologue. Girish Karnad, in his Stage Directions, italicizes the word theatrical. The speech is poetic, stagey and full of grandiose statement:

> Then again I want to climb up, up to the top of the tallest tree in the world, and call out to my people: "Come, my people, I am waiting for you. Confide in me your worries. Let me share your joys. Let's laugh and cry together and then let's pray. Let's pray till our bodies melt and flow and our blood turns into air. History is ours to play with—ours now! Let's be the light and cover the earth with greenery. Let's be darkness and cover up the boundaries of nations. Come! I am waiting to embrace you all! (10)

This is not an address in the Durbar, nor is it a king's message to his citizens on his birthday. The scene takes place in a room in the palace. The only person listening to him is the stepmother. So, no wonder, she laughs and tells him: I can't ask a simple question without your giving a *royal performance*. (Italics mine) (10-11)

The gestures and speech behaviour of Muhammad are theatrical. He plays a "role" now, then changes costumes, and plays another "role." Before Sheik Imam-Ud-Din, he plays the role of a true ruler interested in establishing a "new world." He plays it so well Imam-Ud-Din tells him: "You know, Sultan, I'm just beginning to understand why they saw you are the cleverest man in the world." (24) Scene Six opens with silence. "Muhammad is restless and paces up and down. When the Amirs enter, the restlessness is gone. He welcomes them "with *obvious* warmth." Every emotion is to be shown. It is an actor's responsibility to make things obvious for the audience, either directly or indirectly. The pensive, restless mood is replaced by an imposed cordiality. Like a skilful actor, Muhammad keeps changing roles. Where there is an opportunity, he becomes theatrical in his action also. In Scene Four, when Shihab-Ud-Din perceives Muhammad with a mere bow, Muhammad brings in the actor's touch:

> That's no way to welcome, Shihab. Come—They *embrace.* (Italics mine) (26)

In Scene Six, when he pleads with Amirs to support him in his plans, much to the surprise and embarrassment of the Amirs, he kneels before them. "The Amirs *almost recoil at this sudden gesture.*" (40) They are taken aback by his theatricality. Like an actor winning applause of the audience by an unexpected gesture, Muhammad outsmarts them. We must remember that Muhammad is aware of the conspiracy of the Amirs at this moment. We are told of his knowledge of the conspiracy only later in the play. So, here is a Sultan, who knows that Amirs have come to kill him and yet stagemanages a "play" before them. He could have easily arrested them in the beginning of the scene itself, but he likes to enjoy the climax of the play, and he would love to exhibit before his audience, how he plays the climax. So he allows the call to prayer. When the Amirs step forward to attack him, the Hindu soldiers overpower them. "*While all this is going on, MUHAMMAD goes on praying unconcerned. Only after finishing the prayer does he step down from the throne.*" (41-42) In Scene Eight, Muhammad is given a long poetic monologue which unravels the anguish of a visionary whose vision has fled. He makes the speech dramatic.

Muhammad is an actor-type. In Michael Anderson's words, an actor is:

> a kind of embossed essence of human being. When he is on stage he steps into one role after another and must be on intimate terms with the entire range of human emotions, when he takes off the grease paint he lacks the protective personality that most of us carry around to shield our true nature from the prying eyes of the world; but the need to display and communicate passion which is his stock in trade is not something that can be left behind in the dressing-room along with the wings and the make-up. The actor type is always in search of an audience: all in all he can prove an enthralling but wholly demanding companion, supremely arrogant and yet supremely vulnerable.[2]

In Scene Eight, Muhammad goes to the Fort in search of an audience. He sends for Barani and talks to him. He tells Barani: "When I came here, I felt I *needed an audience*." (Italics mine) (54) He is a "demanding companion" to the young watchman. There is a constant desire for an audience.

Another important image that highlights the relationship between life and theatre is "role-playing." Disguise in *Tughlaq* is a symbol of role playing. The parallel comic plot of Aziz and Aazam and the main plot converge at one point. Muhammad asks Aziz:

> Who are you? How long did you hope to go on fooling us with your masquerade? (79)

Muhammad recognizes a fellow actor in Aziz who is also a genius in "role-playing." When he forgives Aziz, Muhammad says: "I don't know why I am acting like a fool." (83) The various roles played by Aziz—that of a Brahmin, of a victim, and more significantly that of Khalif—are pointers to the fact that Aziz converts life into a stage and goes on with his role-playing. Aziz is Muhammad's "shadow," his "other." He tells Muhammad: "I insist I am your

Majesty's true disciple." (80) Aziz checkmates Muhammad and sends him into "a guffaw." He recognizes the genius of Aziz, forgives him and makes him an officer of the State. What is made very obvious in the case of Aziz, is made subtle in the case of Muhammad. Muhammad also wears masks and disguises himself. There is a basic dialectics in Muhammad's personality: the visionary and the politician; the idealist and the realist. The whole play is a projection of Muhammad's "divided self." U.R. Anantha Murthy rightly observes:

> The whole play is structured on these opposites: the ideal and the real; the divine aspiration and the deft intrigue. Tughlaq is what he is in spite of his self. Knowledge and an intense desire for divine grace. He is aware of the irony of his life when Aziz, the only character in the play who has skilfully used all the schemes of Tughlaq for his own designs, kills Ghiyas-Ud-Din and comes in his guise as a holy messenger of peace to purify the land and revive the banned prayer.[3]

Dr. K.S. Ramamurthy also comments on the divided self:

> He is at once an idealist and crafty politician, a humanist and a tyrant, a man who has murdered sleep and yet not a Macbeth haunted by supernatural solicitations, a man who thinks and broods too much and yet not a Hamlet incapable of action or guilty of delay.[4]

The "divided self," pointed out by Anantha Murthy, has to be seen on the stage. To visualize the "divided self" in terms of "role-playing" is a popular English theatrical device. John Osborne does that in *Luther*. The man behind the revolution is a person in conflict with himself and his parents. Martin's rebellion is a mask that provides him an opportunity to suppress the familial conflict and fight it out in another ground.

In Karnad's *Tughlaq*, Muhammad is at war with himself. He is basically a visionary, a poet and not a ruler. He loves chess, a rose garden and enjoys reading Sadi's poems. He reads the Greeks. He is aware of the "Greek in me." (21) He speaks of his visions—of finding a "new world, a world I had not found in the Arabs or even the Koran." (21) He builds an Utopia in his visions. His visions are like "the visions which lead Zarathustra or the Buddha." (21) He is constantly talking about "tomorrow," "a new future." Muhammad tells the young watchman in Scene Eight:

> Nineteen. Nice Age! An age when you think you can clasp the whole world in your palm like a rare diamond. I was twenty one when I came to Daulatabad first, and built this fort. I supervised the placing of every brick in it and I said to myself, one day I shall build my own history, like this, brick by brick. . . . Suddenly something happened—as though someone had cast a spell. The torch, the gate, the fort and the sky—all melted and merged and flowed in my blood-stream with the darkness of the night. The moment shed its symbols, its questions and answers, and stood naked and calm where the stars throbbed in my veins. I was the earth, was the grass, was the smoke, was the sky. (53)

Barani sees the visionary in Muhammad. He sees him behind the mask. When Muhammad wants to know the cure for the "honeycomb of diseases," Barani prescribes:

> You are a learned man, your Majesty, you are known the world over for your knowledge of philosophy and poetry. History is not made only in statecraft; its lasting results are produced in the ranks of learned men. That's where you belong, your Majesty, in the company of learned men. Not in the market of corpses. (55)

This learned man, the philosopher, Muhammad, speaks through symbols.[5] To him every rose is "an image of Sadi's poems." (64) That is one of the reasons why Muhammad's language is poetic. He has a poet's vision in his heart. He cannot follow Barani's prescription because that means he must give up playing the Sultan:

> I have often thought of that myself—to give up this futile see-saw struggle and go to Mecca. Sit there by the Kaaba and search for the peace which Daulatabad hasn't given me. What bliss! But it isn't that easy. It isn't as easy as leaving the patient in the wilderness because there's no cure for his disease. (55-56)

Muhammad feels that he still has "something to give, something to teach, which may open the eyes of history." (56)

Aziz too has his moment of epiphany. He suddenly realizes that human life is just "bodies eaten-up by corruption," like the Sultan's moment of revelation in the rose-garden. Both Aziz and the Sultan suffer identity crisis. The Sultan, a visionary, deliberately dons the robes of a ruler. He kills his father, kills his conspirators and makes Sheik Imam-Ud-Din a pawn in his game of holding the sceptre to his fist. He plays a tyrant but very often the role slips by and makes him a civil servant. The act of forgiveness is the real Sultan. He is a poet who has compassion and a comprehensive vision to tolerate human weakness. But when he plays the Sultan, he kills mercilessly even his close relatives—his father, his step-mother and Shihab-Ud-Din. The conflict is between the visionary and the ruler and the struggle of Muhammad is to achieve a synthesis between the two. *Tughlaq* is an excellent tragedy that depicts the struggle and failure of a poet who wants to become a ruler, a visionary who desires to establish an Utopia. The struggle becomes significant as it ends in the failure to effect a synthesis between the poet and the ruler and the failure to found a "new world."

NOTES

1. Girish Karnad, *Tughlaq* (OUP, 1972).
2. Michael Anderson, *Anger and Detachment: A Study of Arden,*

Osborne and Pinter (London: Pitman, 1976), p. 22

3. U.R. Anantha Murthy, "Introduction," *Tughlaq*, p. ix.
4. K.S. Ramamurthi, "Some Aspects of Indian Drama in English with Special Reference to *Tughlaq*," *Litcrit*, 5, No. 1 (1979), p. 17.
5. For an insightful comparison with Caligula, read M.K. Naik, "The Limits of Human Power: A Comparative study of *Tughlaq* and Caligula." *Studies in Indian English Literature* (New Delhi: Sterling, 1987).

The Development of Girish Karnad as a Dramatist: *Hayavadana*

SHUBHANGI S. RAYKAR

Karnad's third play *Hayavadana* was published in 1970, exactly six years after *Tughlaq*. Karnad is not a prolific writer and he is very much against writing in haste. Usually the idea of a play incubates in his mind for a long time and it is only when the total action of the play is clearly before his mind's eye, that he starts writing a play. The story of *Hayavadana* comes partly from Thomas Mann's story titled "Transposed Heads," which in turn is based on one of the versions of the story in *Vetal Panchavimshati*.

A brief summary of "Transposed Heads" is as follows. Shridaman, a Brahmin by birth but Vanijya by profession, and Nanda, a cowherd and blacksmith, are very close friends. Shridaman falls in love with Sita whom he happens to see when the two friends are travelling together. Nanda laughs at the idea but agrees to act as a messenger of his friend. Sita accepts the proposal and marries Shridaman. Some months later while Shridaman, Nanda and Sita are travelling together in a cart to a house of Sita's parents they lose track, come across a temple of Kali and take a halt. Shridaman visits the temple alone and, overcome by an incredible urge, offers himself to the goddess as a sacrifice. Nanda goes in search of his friend, finds what has happened and afraid of the charge that he killed his friend because he was in love with Sita and also because he does not want to live without his friend, kills himself. Sita realizes what has happened and prepares to hang herself. The goddess Durga appears in front of her, chides her for her act and grants life to the two dead bodies. Sita, in her excitement, fixes the heads wrongly. Naturally the problem is: Who is her husband? The hermit Kamdaman whose advice is sought decides in favour of Shridaman's head. Nanda's head, therefore, decides to become a hermit. Gradually Shridaman's head begins to control Nanda's body and the body becomes refined. Sita begins to pine for Nanda, so much so that she sets out to meet him carrying Andhak, her baby boy with her. After a strenuous journey, she finds him at a pleasant spot in the forest. They spend the day and the night in heavenly bliss. Next morning Shridaman arrives on the scene. He suggests that they should kill each other in a combat and that Sita should perform sati. Sita thinks that if she lives the life of a widow Andhak's future will be doomed but if she performed sati Andhak will be a sati's son and his social image will improve. So she gives her consent and burns herself on the funeral pyre of her two husbands!

The stories in the *Vetal Panchavimshati* and Somdeva's *Brihatkatha Saritsagar* are basically the same except for a few alterations in the latter, in place names and in the references to the names of the castes of characters. The story is as follows. Prince Dhavala married Madansundari, the daughter of a king named Suddhapata, through the favour of goddess Gauri, in a temple in the city of Shobhavati. Then one day Svetapata, Suddhapata's son, proceeded to his own country along with his sister and her husband. On the way he came to another temple of goddess Gauri. Dhavala went into the temple to pay homage to the goddess. Through some irresistible urge, he cut off his head with a sword which he chanced to see there, and presented it to the goddess. As Dhavala did not come even after waiting for some time Svetapata went inside. When he found out what Dhavala had done he also cut off his own head and offered it to the goddess. Then Madansundari, realizing that her husband and her brother had been away for a long time, went into the temple and saw their dead bodies lying before the goddess and, in great grief, she also began to cut off her own head. Just then the goddess Gauri appeared before her, prevented her from doing so and offered to her what she wanted. Madansundari, naturally, requested the goddess to restore her husband's and her brother's life. The goddess asked her to set their heads on their shoulders. But through excitement she joined her husband's head to her brother's body and vice versa. When they came back to life Madansundari realized her own mistake. Vetala's question is "Who is Madansundari's husband?" The king answers "Of course the person with Dhavala's head on his shoulders."

Karnad's play in a characteristic way begins where the *Vetal* story ends. "How would the woman take it if it really happened and would it ultimately solve the problem for her," are the fascinating problems the artist in him faces. In all his plays Karnad takes this kind of leap from the original story and develops it further. This further development is the play of the artist's imagination and it challenges the glib solutions offered in the original stories. In the story of Yayati as it appears in the Adiparva of the *Mahabharata*, Puru's acceptance of his father's old age smoothly resolves the story. But Karnad's play *Yayati* uses this only as a starting point. If the young Puru had a wife how would she feel about Puru's extraordinary decision, becomes the starting point of his exploration of the problem raised by the mythical story. Something similar happens in his latest play *Atte Ka Kukkut* (translated from Kannada into Hindi but not translated into English so far). In the original story in the Jain Purana on which Karnad has based his play the king is a Jain but his mother is a Hindu. When he relates to her a certain dream that he dreamt she advises him to sacrifice a cock to a goddess. He being a Jain and committed to practice of non-violence in every sphere of life plans to sacrifice instead a cock made of dough. But in Karnad's play the cock comes to life just as it is to be sacrificed and the play develops from that point onwards. Perhaps the problem he wants to raise is, "Can something so serious as one's faith in non-violence be taken so casually? Would not the king accept the idea of violence even if he kills a cock made of dough?" The audience is thus forced to reconsider the glib solution offered in the Purana. In *Hayavadana* what Karnad wants to suggest is that for us King Vikram's solution does not solve the problem. In fact the real problem begins when it appears to be solved. That could be the reason why he dropped the version of *Vetal Panchavimshati* which had the "incest" theme at its core. At the same time he makes significant departures from Thomas Mann's story too. The sub-plot of *Hayavadana* is entirely Karnad's invention. In the play the stories of the sub-plot throughout support the main plot.

Hayavadana is an enigmatic play. Critical opinion is divided about what its main theme is. Kirtinath Kurtkoti who wrote a brief introduction to the English translation published in 1975 says:

> The original play poses a moral problem while Mann uses it to ridicule the mechanical conception of life which differentiates between body and soul. He ridicules the philosophy which holds the head superior to the body. The human body, Mann argues, is a fit instrument for the fulfilment of human destiny.

Karnad's play poses a different problem, that of human identity in a world of tangled relationships.

Another critic U.R. Anantha Murthy in his "A Note of Karnad's *Hayavadana*" has this to say about theme: "The play exposes the audience to a significant theme like 'incompleteness' in a comic mode." A few paragraphs later he says, "The play tries to create an illusion in us that the head determines the being of man."

R.S. Sharma in a lively note says:

> That completeness is a humanly impossible ideal is suggested first in the story of *Hayavadana* and later in the transposition of heads. By showing the absurdity of the ideal of completeness the play finally achieves its aesthetic goal. It implicitly asserts the value and significance of human imperfection which makes any upward movement possible.

To me, the theme of the play has two aspects, a socio-cultural aspect and a metaphysical one. At both levels it shows the conflict between two polarities (namely Appollonian and Dionysian) as the vital truth of human existence. How does one define "completeness" or "perfection?" If perfection or completeness means fusion of the two extreme polarities (at the metaphysical level), the play suggests that such fusion is not possible and this is for the simple reason that if the cycle of nature must continue, it will do so only through a dialectical relationship between Apollonian and Dionysian aspects of life. At the socio-cultural level the play suggests that the Apollonian always asserts itself and subdues the Dionysian in our socio-cultural life. So the co-existence of the two is ruled out (this point is proved later) physically as well as morally. Human society is made possible only through submission to the Apollonian principle. The collective wisdom of society flouts passion (represented in the play by the judgement of the Rishi and Padmini's passion for Kapila respectively). It will bring about the destruction of the individuals who defy order in society. Padmini's predicament is the predicament of a modern, emancipated woman in our society who is torn between two polarities, a woman who loves her husband as well as someone else for two different aspects of their personalities. A civilized Apollonian society and its moral code will not accept such a woman. The two men will not accept each other when it comes to sharing a woman and all the three will destroy themselves in the process.

Devadatta and Kapila's friendship obviously evolves out of their fascination for the aspect which each one of them lacks. They are thus complementary to each other. But the woman whom both of them love is fascinated by both of them and this creates the problem.

Anantha Murthy points out that it is significant that Kapila is a blacksmith—a lower caste in the Hindu caste system while Devadatta is a brahmin. That is why Padmini's fascination for both of them at the same time would be all the more unacceptable to the society in which they live. But this is surely an incidental complication. The real crux of the problem is that society in its present form would not accept a woman living with two men.

Devadatta, the Brahmin and husband, Padmini his wife; and Kapila the low caste, Devadatta's friend but almost like his "dasa," always willing to serve Devadatta and Padmini: this represents the social order. That is why Devadatta's accomplishments which go with the role the social order has imposed on him are so approvingly recounted by Bhagavata.

The first is Devadatta. Comely in appearance, fair in colour, unrivalled in intelligence, Devadatta is the only son of the Revered Brahmin Vidyasagars. Having felled the mightiest pundits of the kingdom in debates on logic and love, having blinded the greatest poets of the world with his poetry and wit, Devadatta is as it were the apple of every eye in Dharamapura. The other youth is Kapila. He is the only son of the ironsmith Lohita, who is to the King's armoury what an axle is to the chariot-wheel. He is dark and plain to look at, yet in deeds which require drive and daring, in dancing, in strength and physical skills, he has no equal

But it is clear that for Padmini who is not at all willing to play docilely the role that society imposes on her and for Kapila who also is impulsive (as can be seen from his climbing the tree the moment Padmini desires to have a flower of the fortunate lady), surely his extraordinary devotion to Devadatta and his constant fawning upon Padmini and calling her sister-in-law are but instances of introverted sublimation of his impulsive Dionysian nature, the "order" imposed by society is destructively restrictive. Devadatta and Kapila accept the restrictions and make a virtue of these restrictions and resort to platitudes such as friendship etc. to make reality bearable. Padmini, "the female principle," more bold, more frank in demanding what will fulfil her— "selfish" in the eyes of Kali— in a daring endeavour tries to get the best of both. But it is clear that Padmini's extra-marital relationship with Kapila or her accepting Kapila as a second husband will threaten the "order" in this society. That all the three die at the end shows that the Apollonian principle ("order") wins. The question that the play poses is: "Are the deaths justifiable?" If they are not justifiable (that they are not justifiable is shown through the handling of the form—comic, grotesque etc.) then obviously there is a need for change in the socio-cultural pattern. There is need of a society which will accept a woman who is in love with two men at one and the same time.

Devadatta and Kapila are close friends. Both love Padmini and yet each recoils from the obvious solution: namely they should both live with Padmini.

Devadatta:	Tell me one thing. Do you really love Padmini?
Kapila:	Yes.
Devadatta:	So do I.
Kapila:	I know. (Silence) Devadatta, could not we all three live together—like Pandavas and Draupadi?
Devadatta:	What do you think? (Silence. Padmini looks at them but does not say anything).
Kapila:	(laughs) No, it cannot be done.
Devadatta:	That is why I brought this. (shows the sword)

They, thus, yield to the Apollonian insistence on the status quo and would prefer to die and to have their beloved Padmini reduced to ashes rather than obey their Dionysian impulses.

Karnad, however, wants to make his audience aware of the inadequacy, indeed futility of such a solution. This he does by making the Bhagavata pose the question directly to the audience. "What? What indeed is the solution to this problem, which holds the entire future of these three unfortunate beings in a balance?"

But it would be worthwhile at this point to see how he has manipulated the characters in the play to prepare the audience for the response he wants from them to the Bhagavata's question.

After the initial episode of the actor and Hayavadana (very much like the "purvaranga" in a "Kirtan" and reminiscent of the dispute over the ownership of the valley which is the opening episode in Brecht's *Caucasian Chalk Circle* which has very important implications for the story which is to unfold) the Bhagavata begins the story of Devadatta, Padmini and Kapila.

By changing their names from the original story or the story by Thomas Mann, Karnad on the one hand makes them generic, that is to say, representative. The name of Devadatta (given by gods) reveals the Apollonian aspect whereas Kapila (dark and therefore earthy) reveals Kapila's Dionysian tendencies. Padmini, like a lotus, seeks to be a delicate bridge between the earth and the sky.

Also like a lotus she is more rooted in the earth and, therefore, has greater affinity for the Dionysian aspect of life manifest in Kapila. Their dilemma has implications for the present-day audience irrespective of their socio-cultural station in life. This device of giving his characters generic names also helps Karnad to dovetail the characters into the Bhagavata's narration, for stories in their oral, narrative style are mostly—since they are designed to drive home a moral—about representative characters. But quite soon we realize that Karnad is intent on endowing them with striking individuality which alone could make their dilemma emotionally, that is to say aesthetically, appealing. Anantha Murthy feels dissatisfied with the play because the playwright, he feels, has not been able to "show" certain facets of the main characters, especially that of Devadatta. He, however, overlooks the facts that Karnad has used a form in which narrative "telling" is vastly more important than it is in a realistic, psychological play. Indeed in this tradition the playwright need not "show" the facts "told" by the narrator, the Bhagavata, as they carry enough weight for the audience not to demand further "showing." But even as the Bhagavata proceeds to "tell" the story the characters as it were insist on coming into their own, insist, that is to say, on living their own lives, and making their own decisions. It is like the puppets in a puppet-dance suddenly insisting on dancing to their own impulses. It is in these parts of the play that Karnad succeeds in making them individuals and since his intention is just to stretch the narrative form that he is using he does not care—indeed he would seriously damage the design of his play if he did—to follow the device to the end and try to "show" the characters unfolding themselves.

Immediately after he sees Padmini, Kapila says to himself, "What she needs is a man of steel." That he is a blacksmith should make it easy for us to discern what Kapila feels about Padmini but he quickly subjugates his feelings to his more representative role; that of a loyal friend who is almost like a *dasa* to Devadatta. Later on when Devadatta decides against going to the picnic, Kapila's individual feelings surface, only to be submerged in the role that he has accepted to play:

So it's off. What am I to do for the rest of the day? What am I to do for the rest of the week? Why should it feel as though one whole world has been wiped out for a whole week? Why this emptiness—Kapila, Kapila, get a tight hold on yourself. You are a slipping boy, control yourself. Don't lose that hold. Go now—don't come here again for a week—Devadatta's bound to get angry with you for not coming. Sister-in-law will be annoyed. But don't come back.

It is true, as Anantha Murthy points out, that Devadatta is the least "individuated" character. But this is explicable in terms of the thematic design of the play. Devadatta is the character around whom the Apollonian order is created. He, therefore, is least subject to passion and, therefore, least impulsive of the three. Even his offering his head to Kali appears to be the end product of a ratiocinative act. Before he offers himself to the goddess Devadatta says, "Good bye Kapila, Good Bye Padmini. May the Lord Rudra bless you. You are two pieces of my heart—live happily together. I shall find my happiness in that."

His generosity and selflessness professed here are forced as the audience knows from the earlier dialogue in the play. Once he realizes the nature of the relationship Padmini and Kapila are heading towards, he decides to remove himself from the scene rather than make the painful choice of sharing Padmini with Kapila.

When Kapila appears on the scene he realizes what Devadatta's "sacrifice" implies. Once again instead of obeying his impulses—which would mean going back to Padmini and taking her away with him—he chooses to do what is expected of him in his role as a "devoted friend" namely kill himself because he cannot live without a friend. He dies asserting, "No Devadatta, I can't live without you. Devadatta, my brother, my father, my friend."

The goddess—who sees and knows everything—is, however, not taken in by these platitudes. She spells out clearly what the audience might have only vaguely felt all along:

> The rascals! They were lying to their last breaths. That fellow Devadatta—he had once promised his head to Rudra and his arms to me! Then because you insisted on going to the Rudra temple he comes here and offers his head. Nobly too—wants to keep his word—No other reason!

This sarcastic statement makes it clear that Devadatta had made his promise to the goddess an "excuse," a noble and acceptable "excuse," for hiding his real motive. The goddess continues:

> This Kapila. Died right in front of me—but "for his friend." And what lies! says he is dying for friendship. He must have known perfectly well he would be accused of killing Devadatta for you. Do you think he would not have grabbed you if it had not been for that fear? No till his last breath—Oh my friend! My dear brother!

Among these three characters it is only Padmini who is courageous enough to defy order and get what she thinks will bring her fulfilment. Kapila grasps the essence of her character. When immediately after he meets her he says, "She is bright like lightning and as sharp."

Unlike Devadatta and Kapila, she refuses to play the role others expect her to play. All through the play Padmini wants to be just herself. She refuses to play the role of the bashful bride on her wedding night. Both Devadatta and Kapila express on different occasions their concern for her condition (she is expecting a baby). But on all occasions she firmly rebukes their bookish concern for her safety and insists on doing what she wants to do. Her uninhibited nature is established right at the beginning of the play through the song of the female chorus: "Why should love stick to the sap of a single body? A head for each breast. A pupil for each eye. A side for each arm. I have neither regret nor shame."

This is asserted again and again in the conversation between Padmini and Devadatta and in the conversation between the goddess and Padmini. Padmini says to the goddess, "If you'd saved either of them I would have been spared all this terror, this agony. Why did you wait so long?"

If Padmini wanted to play the role of a Pativrata (a woman devoted to her husband) she should have opted for Devadatta, suppressing her desire for Kapila. But she does not want to and says so very frankly. The goddess appreciates her frankness and says to her, "Only you spoke the truth—You spoke the truth—because you are selfish."

In fact Padmini wants them both but this would not be acceptable to society and she knows exactly what she wants from each of them. She wants Devadatta's mind and Kapila's physicality while society forces her to seek these qualities, if she can, in one man. She would like "a perfect man" who possesses both these aspects of human personality whom she, as it were, creates in her excitement by transposing the heads of Devadatta and Kapila. The goddess once again discerns her motives and says in a resigned tone, "My dear daughter, there should be a limit even to honesty" and adds "anyway so be it!"

One must choose one's course of action and then accept the consequences unflinchingly. But if understood as a deliberately chosen one Padmini's act is ultimately a consequence of the social norms imposed on her. Since she cannot have both Devadatta and Kapila she tries to get past the norms by having what she most wants from each of them. But this does not at all solve the problem.

The second act of *Hayavadana* is largely Karnad's creation for he develops it from a question that he asks himself as he arrives at the end of a traditional story. His development of the second act is based to a greater extent on the story by Thomas Mann but the conclusions offered are to be interpreted differently. The second act shows that the solution Vikrama gave to the problem is inadequate in the present situation. Padmini's act of going with Devadatta's head is based on the solution of the Rishi who in fact reiterates King Vikram's solution. But if the head controls the body it logically follows that it will transform the body. That is what happens and so far as Padmini is concerned she again remains with Devadatta, her husband. Worse still she is forced to watch the transformation taking place and thus lose Kapila bit by bit. Ultimately she finds herself faced with the same problem which faced her in the first act. She misses Kapila, his impulsiveness and his physicality all the more because she has tested it more intimately through Devadatta's head and Kapila's body in the early days (after the metamorphosis).

In the first act the supernatural element that is the goddess Kali is used to reveal conscious motives behind the actions of the three protagonists. Here he uses the animate dolls as a device to report to us from moment to moment what is going on in Padmini's mind. Her psychological reaction to the transformation in Devadatta is very economically communicated. The sense of time passing is also given by making the dolls report to each other what Padmini dreams, what reveries she indulges in. They also "feel" the change taking place in Devadatta:

> Doll I: His palms! They were so rough, when he first brought us here. Like a labourer's. But now they are soft—sickly soft—like a young girl's . . .
>
> Doll II: His stomach. It was so tight and muscular. Now . . .

Karnad also uses the dolls as a "device" in the development of the plot. It is because the dolls get old that Padmini can send Devadatta to the Ujjain fair. He could have used the Bhagavata to narrate what is going on in Padmini's mind. But that would have affected his success in making her character individuated and generic (representative) at one and the same time. She, then, would have been more of a representative and less of an individuated character. The Bhagavata has deeper knowledge of Padmini's nature. He knows what kind of person she is, as is clear from his comments when Padmini and Kapila meet in the forest:

> And as I saw him change I could not get rid of you. That's what Padmini must tell Kapila. She should say more without concealing anything: "Kapila, if that Rishi had given me to

you, would I have gone back to Devadatta some day exactly like this?" But she doesn't say anything. She remains quiet.

The Bhagavata knows Padmini and therefore he knows what must be going on in her mind. (He is partly like the omniscient narrator.) The dolls on the contrary have only a limited knowledge of Padmini because they are endowed by the dramatist with a special vision (Divyadrishti) which can make them see and only "see" what is going on in the mind of Padmini. It is indeed a very ingenious device.

Padmini tries to act rationally when she first senses the transformation in Devadatta. "I am not going to be stupid again. Kapila has gone out of my life for ever. I won't let him come back again." She, however, is not the one who can act rationally. She yields to the impulse all too soon. Once she knows that her husband can only be Devadatta, he cannot be Kapila, there is an urge in her to accept "Kapila—the—person." So far she knew only "Kapila's body" now she wants to know Kapila the person. When Devadatta goes to the Ujjain fair to buy new dolls for the child, she suddenly, on an impulse, undertakes a strenuous journey carrying the child with her and because he has been taught to accept social norms adds, "Devadatta and Padmini! Devadatta and Padmini! A pair coupled with the holy fire as witness. I have no place there, no peace, no salvation. Go on, I beg you, Go."

Padmini, however, has realized that she must accept Kapila "totally." Kapila's body which was once Devadatta's body knows Padmini intimately. His head also must know her. That will give "completeness" to Kapila.

When Devadatta appears on the scene with swords and he and Kapila decide to fight he says: "No grounds for friendship now. No question of mercy. We must fight like lions and kill like cobras." He, through his experience of having lived with "Kapila's body" has learnt that the talk about generosity, mercy and friendship with which he hid his subconscious motives earlier is now meaningless. Both Kapila and he accept that both of them living together with Padmini is not possible so long as they live. The only alternative is to kill each other which they do in "resignation."

Padmini prepares to perform "Sati." The very idea of "Sati" is ridiculed here. The song of the female chorus is full of grotesque beauty:

> Female Chorus: The fortunate lady's procession goes to the street of laburnums, while the makarandas tie the pennants and jacarandas hold lights. Good-bye, dear sister. Go without fear. The Lord of death will be pleased with the offering of three coconuts.

It keeps the audience detached from any kind of emotional involvement with the "sad-scene." The audience, as a result, thinks dispassionately about Padmini's death. Padmini's choice of death allows her to assert her will through death. She would have liked to assert it even when she was alive; but she could not, partly because of the social norms and partly due to the realization that her accepting two husbands, namely Kapila and Devadatta, would not solve the problem so long as they themselves could not reconcile themselves to the idea. Padmini solves her problem in an existential fashion. As she dies she says to the Bhagavata:

> My son is sleeping in the hut. Take him under your care. Give him to the hunters who live in this forest and tell them it's Kapila's son. They loved Kapila and will bring the child up. Let the child grow in the forest with rivers and trees. When he's five take him to the Revered Brahmin Vidyasagar of Dharampura. Tell him it's Devadatta's son.

So the fusion of the Dionysian and Apollonian is Padmini's dream which she wants to be fulfilled through her son.

But Padmini and Devadatta's choice of death affects the child's growth adversely. "This child doesn't laugh, doesn't cry, doesn't even smile. There's obviously something wrong with him," as the actor puts it.

The stories of the plot and sub-plot lead thus to the same

conclusion. Hayavadana's mother, the princess of Karnataka, sought to be a mare and galloped away without thinking in the least of Hayavadana, the product of her marriage with the white stallion. Padmini's act runs parallel to the story of Hayavadana's mother. Hayavadana is thrown into this world neither a beast nor a human being. Padmini's son becomes totally withdrawn from the world, "autistic." The inanimate "dolls" are his only companions—in fact they are the ones he knows intimately in this world. When he meets Hayavadana his innocent smile makes Hayavadana a complete horse and Hayavadana's laughter makes the boy forget his dolls and his regressive tendencies. It makes the child's return to humanity possible. They, thus, cease to suffer from the consequences of the acts of their parents. But this happy ending of a comedy does not prevent the audience from thinking over the other existential problem presented through the story of Kapila, Padmini and Devadatta. Padmini asserts her choice through death, Hayavadana's mother asserts hers through becoming a mare. Both Padmini's son and Hayavadana do not have a choice in the matter. They are brought into this world and they suffer as a result of the parents's act. Is the act of their parents justified?

At this point Karnad makes a very significant change in the story he borrowed from Mann. In Mann's "Transposed Heads" Sita dies thinking that her performing "Sati" will improve the image of her son in society and the son does become a good scholar and a reader to the king of Benares, unlike Padmini's who is autistic and withdrawn.

It now remains to consider a few more formal features of the play. The play borrows heavily from the Yakshagana and many other folk forms. Karnad's contribution is that he introduces (a relatively unknown and partly original) story which a folk form would normally avoid. Karnad had not employed folk theatre devices on such an extensive scale earlier. It is likely that Karnad felt that in the "naturalistic form" the play would never achieve the "universalization" of the theme the way it achieves it in its present form. The "non-naturalistic" form as Karnad employs it is very close to Brecht's Epic theatre. A narrator is used both in Karnad's play as well as in Brecht's Epic theatre. Both make extensive use of songs and music. In both there is linear and loose plot construction avoiding climax and revelation. Actors wear masks in both and in both again the action is presented largely through "miming." This makes the "universal framework" easier. It also succeeds in making the audience think about the problem in a more detached manner. One does not know whether the choice of the form determines the choice of the story or vice versa, but Karnad's choice of a folk tale for his play is very apt because it lifts the play above limitations of time and place.

Karnad has successfully managed to present his characters as "representatives" in spite of having made them highly individuated in some sections of the play and the names given to the characters are generic and suggestive as we have already seen.

The dialogue of the play is at once neutral and contemporary and helps to give contemporaneity to the problem the play discusses. For example:

Devadatta: It's humour for you. It burns my insides.
Padmini: Aw, Shut up. Don't I know how liberal and large hearted you are? You are not the sort to get jealous.

Karnad's use of the character of the Bhagavata contributes a lot to the formal aspect (achievement) of the play. He does not merely borrow the character of Bhagavata from a typical Yakshagana play. He increases the scope of the role by making the Bhagavata not a mere commentator-narrator but also by making him one of the characters. The scene between the Bhagavata and Kapila before Padmini reaches Kapila's hut and the scene between the Bhagavata and Padmini when she prepares to perform "Sati" are good examples of it. This helps him achieve in a play what Mann achieves in the story through the third person narrator.

The supernatural, i.e. the goddess, is also used as a device. She is "terrible" in appearance but is given all the characteristics of a human being. She is angry at the thought that Devadatta should promise his "head" to Rudra and only his "arms" to her. She is vexed when aroused from her sleep. Through the use of this device Karnad asserts that there are no ready-made solutions for human problems. The solution offered by the goddess is no solution. She only does what she is asked to do and allows Padmini to carry on her mistake even when she has seen through Padmini's honesty. In short the problem is unresolved and will be solved only through human effort, i.e., by changing the relationships and concepts of relationships which can be done only by the human beings themselves.

One of the striking features of *Hayavadana* is the introduction of the device of making inanimate objects animate. This is a frequent feature in folk literature but not in folk drama. The device, also like the device of Bhagavata, helps Karnad to prove the psychological reality of the characters in the dramatic form which was achieved through the narrator in Mann's story. He has used the female chorus which is absent in the Yakshagana play. The ludicrous song given to the female chorus when Padmini performs "Sati" has already been discussed. In addition to these masks, the songs, the half curtains and the painted curtains, verbalization of the situation through narration, the continuation of the action without any formal break-up of scenes, the total absence of the front curtain are all devices carefully used to create the effect of alienation.

The most remarkable feature of the play from this point of view is that the entire action of the play is "mimed." This was not done either in *Yayati* or *Tughlaq*. It achieves universalization of the problem to a remarkable degree. Highly individualized subtle emotions cannot be communicated through miming. Fine shades of a particular emotion can be conveyed through soliloquies. In the naturalistic theatre the entire focus is sometimes on a single character and the character is allowed to reveal subtle emotions through the speech given to it and mostly through facial expressions. The speech given to Liubov Andryeevna in *The Cherry Orchard* Act II is a case in point.

> L. Andryeevna: Oh, my sins! Look at the way I've always squandered money, continually. It was sheer madness. And

then I got married to a man who only knew how to get into debt. Champagne killed him—he was a terrific drinker—and the worse luck, I fell in love with someone else. We had an affair, and just at that very time it was my first punishment, a blow straight to my heart—my little boy was drowned here, in this river . . . and then I went abroad. I went away for good, and never meant to return. I never meant to see the river again, I just shut my eyes and ran away in a frenzied grief, but he, he followed me. It was so cruel and brutal of him! I bought a villa near Mentone because he fell ill there, you see, and for three years I never had any rest, day or night. He was a sick man, he quite wore me out; my soul seemed to dry right up. Then last year when the villa had to be sold up to pay the debts. I went to Paris, and there he robbed me and left me; he went away and lived with another woman. . . . I tried to poison myself. It was all so foolish, so shameful! and then suddenly I felt an urge to come back to Russia, to my own country and my little girl . . . (wipes away her tears.) Oh Lord, Lord, be merciful, forgive me my sins, don't punish me anymore! (Takes a telegram out of her pocket.) I had this from Paris, today. He's asking my forgiveness, begging me to return. (Tears up the telegram) Sounds like music somewhere. (Listens).

Sometimes the conversation may go on between two characters revealing the interplay of subtle emotions. The dramatist himself suggests through stage directions how the actors should reveal this play of emotions with the help of facial expression. The conversation between Hilde and Solnes in the first act of *The Master Builder* is a good example of this. These function somewhat like the close-up in the film. There is no scope for all this when the entire action is mimed. "Miming," thus is the most important feature of the play so far as the "alienation effect" is concerned.

Experiment and Innovation in Modern Indian Drama in Translation: The Plays of Mohan Rakesh, Badal Sircar, Vijay Tendulkar and Girish Karnad

VEENA NOBLE DASS

Modern Indian drama reveals two main tendencies, both natural to a historical development. One is, Indian playwrights have gone back to tradition for their themes and techniques and the other is, making use of what are considered modern trends in the theatre. These two tendencies are specially seen in theatrical events in the 1960s and 1970s which led to an unconscious awareness of the oneness or "Indianness" of Indian theatre, though such terms as Hindi theatre, Bengali theatre, Marathi theatre or Kannada theatre are still used.

Plays written in various Indian languages are being translated into English and other languages as they are produced and appreciated in the various parts of the country. A closer contact is being established between the theatre workers from different regions and languages through these translations.

Thus regional drama in India is slowly paving a way for a "national theatre" into which all streams of theatrical art seem to converge. The major language theatres that are active all through the turbulent years of rejuvenation and consolidations are those of Hindi, Bengali, Marathi and Kannada. Not that there are less number of great dramatists in other areas, or less important dramatic activity in other languages, but these four have initiated in the fifties and sixties, a new experimental theatre which has cross-cultural manifestations. They also paved the way for the emergence of important writers in these four major languages.

A brief study of a few of these, namely Mohan Rakesh, Vijay Tendulkar, Badal Sircar and Girish Karnad, shows clearly that they are the children of the new resurgence in their own areas and have established that, by translating and performing the translated plays in other language areas than their own, they are marching towards the possibility of building a national theatre movement. Hence a study of these four representative writers becomes inevitable to students of culture in general and students of drama in particular, if they want to know how the contemporary Indian drama has made bold innovations and fruitful experiments which go in the history of Indian drama as a significant mark of achievement.

Mohan Rakesh was one of those rare literary personalities who never accept the traditional set up but always aspire to find and project something which is challenging and new. Rakesh's language separates him from other Hindi playwrights and puts him on a higher level of competence. His plays—*Ashadh Ka Ek Din* (One Day in Ashadha),[1] *Lehron Ke Rajhans*[2] (Great Swans of the Waves), *Adhe-adhure*[3] (Half-way House)—show that his dialogues have a smooth flow, a meaningful depth and an elemental naturalness suitable to his characters. They express the characters's mental conflict, frustration, dissatisfaction and the resulting anger in a unique manner. Though some of the dialogues between Mallika and Kalidasa in *One Day in Ashadha* tend to be longer than required and seem to be a little heavy on the audience, they are necessary to the play. As Kalidasa says in the play, "people think that living in that life and atmosphere I have written a great deal. But I know that while living there I wrote nothing. Whatever I wrote was a recollection of life here."[4] This lengthy dialogue is necessary for the reader to understand the feelings and moods of the characters. But Rakesh became conscious of this and made an effort to reduce the lengths of the dialogues in his other plays namely *The Great Swans of the Waves* and *Half-way House*. Though in the former play, the dialogues between Nand and Sundari tend to become longer, in *Half-way House* the playwright seems to be completely in control of the situation. Here the dialogues are short, suitable and to the point. They hit at the subject immediately. It cannot be denied that

Rakesh contributed much to the enrichment of the language.

One aspect of his plays is that he pays much attention to the internal conflict in the minds of his characters. He has made an effort to come to grips with the problem of man-woman relationship. The irony and tragedy of this problem on different levels has been treated in his plays. Nand, Kalidasa, Man I in *One Day in Ashadha, Great Swans of the Waves* and *Half-way House* run away from Sundari, Mallika and Savitri respectively. But do they succeed in doing so? Neglected by man and left alone are Mallika, Sundari, and Savitri but are they able to face the new situation? These are the problems that Mohan Rakesh tackled in his plays. The depiction of the complexity of the human heart, man's helplessness and the chains of relationship attract the audience and keep them enthralled.

Rakesh's technique of taking support from historical themes and then throwing light on the realities of life is quite his own. He has his own style of saying what he wants to say. He himself has explained the dilemma of this problem by saying that to some people the word "contemporary" has meaning only in terms of consciousness. But he really was not aware of having written anything that is not contemporary because history as such has fascinated him much for creative interpretation. Therefore this technique would be understood only by those who knew that in the context of creative writing the meaning of the word "contemporary" is not the same as in journalism.

It may however be argued as to why a writer should choose the historical or semi-historical background for interpreting contemporary life. To this Rakesh replies: "I know the force of this argument and can only say that I have no prejudice in the matter. I do mean to write plays with a contemporary background, but the point I wish to emphasize is that background itself is no criterion."[5]

While Rakesh used historical characters to project the breakdown of communication, Badal Sircar, the great Bengali playwright uses contemporary situations and social problems to project the life-in-death attitude of modern life. The central theme of many of his early plays is a sense of utter meaninglessness in our existence which leads to a state of metaphysical anguish.

This anguish is in fact closely embedded in the Bengali middle-class psyche, the tearing up of which was Sircar's constant concern since his early theatre career. It is an irony that early Bengali drama of the mid-nineteenth century has strong social moorings, but could not lead the middle-class man towards a self-awareness. The drama of 1880s bears testimony to this attitude of the middle-classes towards social responsibility.

Sircar's early plays *Evam Indrajit*[6] (And Indrajit), *Baki Itihas*[7] (The Other Side of History) and *Sheish Nei*[8] (There is No End) are based on political, social and psychological problems. *And Indrajit* is about the residue of the middle class who have failed to adjust, align and cease to aspire among the intellectually alive urban middle-class.

And Indrajit was not the only play written by Sircar when he was away from India. A particularly prolific period in his play-writing career occurred between 1966 and 1967 when he wrote six plays while working as a town-planner in Nigeria. Three of these plays are *Bagh*[9] (Tiger) *Jadi Aur Ekbar*[10] (If there were other Chances) and *Pralap*[11] (Mad Speech). Though these plays are not inconsequential, they are far from what Sircar believes is his central concern as a playwright, nothing less exciting than "the responsibility of mankind for the events of our times."[12] The horror of Hiroshima, in particular, obsessed Sircar in two of his plays—*The Other Side of History* and *There is No End.*

These plays are not only stylistically similar but have a thematic continuity. The framework within which this act of synthesis is made possible is a strong sense of the frustration of the intellectual aspiration, the failure to get involved and the resultant feeling of guilt. The self-surging of the heroes might often provoke discomfort among the readers or the audience. But it is more the chill of being forced to look at something asked, in which they often discover themselves than any strong feeling of embarrassment.

The plays after all the ruthless exposure of responsibility for guilt in personal and social relations end with feeble apologies for a continuation of the conventional mode of living. Perhaps Sircar wants to leave his heroes to suffer from the awareness of the responsibility. He seems to prefer a sort of self-flagellation to any positive action. A lifelong nagging reminder of guilt can be the only consolation for the Indrajits, Sharadindus and Sumantas, who are too sensitive and individualistic to choose any path of action to put an end to Hiroshimas.

These questions, which are difficult to answer, Sircar continues to grapple with in his exploration of the *Third Theatre.*[13] The Third Theatre is an outcome of his interest in involving himself in theatre. Not satisfied with being a playwright, Sircar wanted to do "theatre." He was at this time influenced by his tours to U.S.A. and Czechoslovakia. Sircar's "Satabdi" was the first group in the Bengali theatre that recognized the validity of a "poor" theatre. Grotowski's concept of the need to renounce all outward technique and concentrate on analyzing the closeness of the living organism struck a synonymous chord in Sircar's imagination. His theatre gradually minimized its use of sets, costumes, background, music, tape recorders and projectors. The body of the actor and its relation to the space on stage were Sircar's most immediate concern as a director. Sircar also attempted to break down barriers in theatrical time and space by emphasizing the simultaneous action of his play and its non-sequential mode of narration.

Along with *Spartacus,*[14] Sircar's later plays *Micchil*[15] (Procession), *Bhoma* and *Basi Khabar*[17] (Stale News) are based on the concepts of Third Theatre. *Procession* is one of Sircar's most intricately structured plays with innumerable transactions and juxtapositions. The relentless flow of events in the text is most skillfully concretized in the choreographic movement of the scenes. The actors are constantly on the move, walking, running, dancing and jogging through the room. The benches in the room are placed in such a way that the spectators feel that they are part of a maze. Sircar creates a most bewildering environment with the bodies, backs, faces and profiles of the spectators. When the actors begin to move between and around the environment created by the spectators, the effect is startling. One can almost see a procession winding its way around the streets in Calcutta.

These plays of Sircar have placed him on a pedestal higher than other contemporary playwrights of Indian drama. His time of entry into Indian drama was very appropriate. Perhaps he made the final breakthrough when a considerable amount of modernity had already been ushered in and the new directors who responded so happily to him had already achieved an identity.

In his first three plays the protagonists are all writers, searching for plots to write their stories. This is Sircar's own search for plots to write his plays. But the characters in his later plays which were written after he formulated his Third Theatre are not individualized at all. They can be seen as what Sircar himself has said, "I can be taken as a prototype of a particular class in a society at a particular period."[18] The spectator assumes a protagonist's role in the theatre of Sircar, making the theatrical incident experimental, indeterminative and open-ended.

There are three strands in Badal Sircar's life which mesh well to give a striking texture to his work and introduce a new value to Indian theatre. These strands are his professional career as an urban planner, plus his training as a civil engineer, his inner life as a playwright and its outward expression in his role as a theatre director and actor. More than writing, Sircar prefers doing theatre. This he wants to accomplish by what he said "trekking to the villages and rural areas"[19] in the near future. Sircar wants to go from village to village even to the remotest of them and do theatre and at the same time involve the people. If there is any playwright in the contemporary Bengali theatre who is capable of creating a genuine people's theatre, a theatre supported and created by the people and not merely performed by the people, it is Badal Sircar.

While Badal Sircar makes the society, specially the middle-class, feel guilty for being indifferent towards man and his problems, Vijay Tendulkar, the avant-garde Marathi playwright, harps upon the theme of isolation of the individual and his confrontation with the hostile surroundings. Both these playwrights express their anguish at the prevailing social condition and the role man has to play in these conditions.

Tendulkar stands on a different pedestal from that of the other contemporary Marathi playwrights because of his innovations of style in presenting a large variety of themes. Most of Tendulkar's full-length plays which concentrate on the travails of the little man essay a more or less conventional dramatic form. The plays *Shantata Court Chaloo Aahe*[20] (Silence! The Court is in Session), *Giddh*[21] (Vultures), *Sakharam Binder*[22] and *Ghasiram Kotwal*,[23] which made Tendulkar a popular playwright, are experiments of an intense and deeper impulse and not just a matter of superficial innovation. A kind of new freedom and conviction is seen in these plays. The phrase "sex and violence" is very loosely attributed to in the discussion of these plays. But in none of these, the theme of sex and violence is superficial, as it forms an important part of the content of the plays. These four plays are considered as representative plays of the Marathi theatre of cruelty. Many of Tendulkar's plays show his concern for modern man's anguish. That these plays, so different in content and form, are pointed towards an important human predicament is itself a tribute to the questioning, probing spirit of Tendulkar. The controversies that arose after the performance of many of his plays is a clear proof of his unconventional attitude towards human problems. The theme of violence pervades quite blatantly in most of his plays. Tendulkar was influenced by Artaud's idea of relating the theme of anguish to the theme of violence.

When he was awarded a fellowship by Nehru Memorial Fund Committee, Tendulkar elaborated the theory of violence in his project "Emerging Pattern of Violence," structuring his theory on the concept of the theatre of cruelty. He does not consider the occurrence of human violence as something loathsome or ugly as it is innate in human nature.

Ever since he wrote *Silence! The Court is in Session*, Tendulkar has discovered that violence makes man fascinating and there are many variations in the way violence manifests itself in the way man expresses it. Its various manifestations and how they are moulded by each person are important for a study of human nature. He believes that violence is a basic quality.[24] When this understanding of human nature is translated into a play, it not only becomes an explosive piece of art but a thesis. Tendulkar unabashedly presents and defends it. According to him the most important point is to keep the violence raw while depicting it on stage, not to dress it up with any fancy trapping and not to make it palatable.

Unlike Badal Sircar and Vijay Tendulkar who delved into the problems of the middle-class man, Girish Karnad, the noted Kannada playwright, went back to myths and legends and made them a vehicle of a new vision. By using these myths, he tried to show the absurdity of life with all its elemental passions and conflicts and man's eternal struggle to achieve perfection.

Karnad has won an all-India recognition with his plays *Yayati*,[25] *Tughlaq*,[26] *Atte Ka Kukkut*[27] (The Dough Cock) and *Hayavadana*.[28] He has been in the west and has been attracted by the drama of Giradoux, Anouilh, Camus and Sartre in his search for new forms of drama. Yet he is essentially in the Kannada tradition. His reworking of myths, Puranic, historical and literary, relates him to Kailasam and Rangacharya as much as it does to those European dramatists who remake their myths.

Karnad in his plays tries to evolve a symbolic form out of a tension between the archetypal and mythic experience and a living response to life and its values. Contemporaneity in Karnad's plays manifests itself through his operative sensibility in his attempt to give new meaning to the past from the vantage point of the present.

Karnad does not take the myths in their entirety. He takes only parts of them that are useful to him and the rest he supplements with his imagination to make his plots clear. Thus in *Yayati* he has taken the myth partially. The characters in *Tughlaq* particularly Barani, Najib, Aziz and the stepmother are seen in a new context. In *Hayavadana* the discussion between Devadutta and Kapila is at variance with the myth. Karnad has read extensively Shakespeare, Brecht, Anouilh, Camus, Sartre and to a considerable extent, Pinter, and is influenced by them.

Structurally, the plays offer interesting studies. *Yayati* is the best in this respect. Every character is fully realized and has a clear solidity. This cannot be said of all the characters in *Tughlaq*. Except for Tughlaq and Aziz there is hardly any character that is growing. *Yayati* takes place between sunset and sunrise. *Tughlaq* is in the epic scenes and takes place in a period of five years or more. *Hayavadana* takes place in several years.

There is one drawback in Karnad's characters. All of them are intelligent. There is hardly any who is less than intelligent. Aziz and Tughlaq appear as one. There is nothing that really makes them what they are individually. Individuality is missing. This defect is seen in Devadutta and Kapila also. They lack an individuality that is theatrically essential to their characters holding sustained interest. We see them as chess pieces moved to definite purposes by the playwright.

However Karnad remains undoubtedly the most important dramatist of the contemporary Kannada stage. He has given the Kannada Theatre a richness that could probably be equated only with his talents as an actor-director. He has shown the Indian stage as to what depths the mythical themes could be taken to in order to recreate a contemporary consciousness. Karnad's advantages are many—his expert knowledge of contemporary European theatre, his exposure to the Western dramatic literature and more importantly his theatrical sensibility—all these certainly sharpened by his thorough knowledge of the stage. He has shown to the Indian theatre community and to the world theatre community how our past and present can coalesce to give to our present day existence meaning and to theatre activity a direction.

Thus we find that today when the modern Indian playwright wants to express himself all existing dramatic forms fail him. This necessitates him to find a new form and this urge induces him to begin the search of all traditional theatre forms in his own state or elsewhere. This forces him to examine all the aspects of the folk and classical tradition where it was not difficult to find answers to his questions but the real difficulty was to synthesize them in order to create a new form. What the modern playwright has achieved is a thorough synthesis of all the three traditions—classical, folk and contemporary western, which when used discriminatingly and intelligently, leads to a discovery of a new form and as a result a new style of production—leading to the evolution of "Indian" drama.

NOTES

1. Mohan Rakesh, *One Day in Ashadha*, trans. Sarab K. Ehslay, *Enact*, No. 32-33 (Aug.-Sept. 1969).
2. Mohan Rakesh, *The Great Swans of the Waves*, trans. Paul Jacob and Meena Williams, *Enact*, No. 73-74 (Jan.-Feb. 1973).
3. Mohan Rakesh, *Half-way House*, trans. Bindu Batra, *Enact*, No. 53 (May 1971).
4. *One Day in Ashadha.*
5. Mohan Rakesh, "Why Plays," *Enact*, No. 13-14 (Jan.-Feb. 1968). Unpaginated.
6. Badal Sircar, *Evam Indrajit*, trans. Girish Karnad (Calcutta, Oxford University Press, 1974).
7. Badal Sircar, *Baki Itihas*, trans. Vinod L. Doshi, *Enact*, No. 165-166 (Sept./Oct. 1980).
8. Badal Sircar, *Sheish Nei*, trans. K. Raha, *Enact*, No. 59 (Nov. 1971).
9. Badal Sircar, *Bagh* (Tiger). Not translated into English.
10. Badal Sircar, *Jadi Aur Ekbar*. Not translated into English.
11. Badal Sircar, *Pralap*. Not translated into English.
12. Rustum Barucha, *Rehearsals of Revolution* (Seagull Books, Calcutta, 1983), p. 138.
13. Badal Sircar, *The Third Theatre*, published by Badal Sircar (Calcutta, 1978).
14. Badal Sircar, *Spartacus*, Not translated into English.
15. Badal Sircar, *Michhil* (Procession), trans. Samik Bandyopadhyay, from *Three Plays* (Seagull Books, Calcutta, 1983).
16. Badal Sircar, *Bhoma*, trans. Badal Sircar and Kalyani Ghosh, from *Three Plays*.
17. Badal Sircar, *Bashi Khabar* (Stale News), trans. Samik Bandyopadhyay, from *Three Plays*.
18. Badal Sircar, "Azad Memorial Lectures," 1982, quoted by Ella Dutta in the Introduction to *Three Plays*, p. v.
19. Veena N. Dass, "An Interview with Sircar," Hyderabad, 1985. Unpublished.
20. Vijay Tendulkar, *Silence! The Court is in Session*, trans. Priya Adarkar (Calcutta: Oxford University Press, 1978).
21. Vijay Tendulkar, *The Vultures*, trans. Priya Adarkar (Delhi, Hind

Pocket Books, 1974).

22. Vijay Tendulkar, *Sakharam Binder*, trans. Shanta Shahane and Kumud Mehta (Delhi: Hind Pocket Books, 1973).
23. Vijay Tendulkar, *Ghasiram Kotwal*, trans. Jayant Kurve and Eleanor Zellot (Calcutta: Seagull Books, 1984).
24. Veena N. Dass, "Interview with Tendulkar," (Bombay: 1984). Unpublished.
25. Girish Karnad, *Yayati*, trans. into Hindi by S.R. Narayana (Manohar Granth Mala, Dharwad, 1978).
26. Girish Karnad, *Tughlaq*, trans. Girish Karnad (Delhi: Oxford University Press, 1971).
27. Girish Karnad, *Atte Ka Kukkut*. Not translated into English.
28. Girish Karnad, *Hayavadana*, trans. Girish Karnad (Calcutta: Oxford University Press, 1975).

Domesticity and Drama: An Analysis of Nissim Ezekiel's *Marriage-Poem* and *Don't Call It Suicide*

VRINDA NABAR

I would like to begin my very brief analysis with a few qualifications, in order to define the limits of my study. Ezekiel's first plays were written in the 1960s, while the more recent ones have appeared after a gap of twenty years or more. What one has heard indicates that this second phase still continues. Besides the play *Don't Call It Suicide* (also known as *Soft and Sad Music)* which was staged recently and received some critical attention, Ezekiel is reported to be revising the manuscripts of some more dramatic works.

The sporadic nature of Ezekiel's dramatic output and the fact that, taken as a whole, it does not add up to more than a few plays, make me respond to it in a somewhat guarded manner. I do not think it possible, for instance, to consider seriously his "development" as a dramatic writer, for this would imply a record of sustained creativity, not borne out by the available evidence.

Ezekiel himself would appear to subscribe to this view. In an interview (*Literature Alive,* vol. 1, no. 3, December 1987) he says; "I have not yet written plays substantial enough to be considered in terms of bad, good, better, best and worst . . . *Nalini* and *Marriage-Poem* I consider worth staging."

Patrick Beck, who directed the second of these plays in Bombay not so very long ago, is far more emphatic in this respect: "It is a director's play all the way," he is reported to have said of *Marriage-Poem.* Beck even characterized Ezekiel's theatre as "modern drama all the way." "In France we have a theatre movement today called *Theatre de Quotidienne* or *Theatre of Daily*

Life. It presents the banal, mundane, even dull existence of common people who go about their lives quietly, monotonously. Ezekiel's plays remind me of this kind of movement."

Such glib categorizing, however, is precisely what I feel one should guard against, because there is no corresponding corpus of work that would support such a statement. I would prefer instead, given their fitful appearance, to regard Ezekiel's plays as no more than a very modest contribution to the Indo-English dramatic scene.

Of the *Three Plays* published by Writer's Workshop in the 1960s *Nalini* has generally been regarded as the most successful. To me, however, the play has always seemed limited by the very limited world it portrays. It is interesting as a glimpse of a slice of life, perhaps, but would have been more so if Ezekiel's dramatic output had been more prolific so that what was witnessed here was part of a wider spectrum. If the function of drama is chiefly to represent, then *Nalini* performs its limited function adequately. But it is too isolated a reality, one that holds only a marginal interest. To me *Marriage-Poem* is more representational and therefore more satisfying as theatre.

Marriage-Poem is not an "ambitious" play. Its theme and treatment are in the mode of conventional theatre. These are defining statements, not negative comments. What I mean is that the theme of the play—a marriage that is clearly disharmonious—is presented in a fairly straightforward manner. There are no elaborate attempts to superimpose, formally, any philosophies of drama or theatre, merely because they are fashionable abroad. There is no deliberate *avant-gardeism*, just as there is no fake existentialism, sense of alienation, etc. Nor is there any strenuous attempt to "modernize" the technique, which remains that of conventional theatre for the most part.

The playwright develops our perception of a failed marriage through several devices. The stage directions, occasionally elaborate and wordy, generally brief but precise, underscore the fact that this is drama and should be treated as such. They leave little room for ambiguity in one's visual conception of a scene. This is important because *Marriage-Poem* is a series of shifting scenarios.

The dramatic emphasis is obvious enough in the various Naresh-Mala exchanges. I would however prefer to illustrate with the example of a very small scene, significant enough in the action. Structurally it has all the nuances of a dream-sequence, since it does not logically fit into the sequential pattern of events. At the same time, it depicts a crucial aspect of the marriage—the husband's romantic involvement with another woman who gives him the sympathy and companionship he does not (or thinks he does not) find in his wife.

On stage, the lights "dim quickly, brighten slowly" to reveal Leela, the 'other woman.' "Naresh rushes up to her, they embrace ecstatically":

Leela: *(Ruffling his hair)* O, my poor boy.
Naresh: *(Disengaging)* Don't pity me.
Leela: I ran half the way from the station. My train stopped between stations over and over again.
Naresh: O, they do that, but they make up time, somehow.
Leela: Mine didn't. It was ten minutes late.
Naresh: Ten minutes. That's not very long.
Leela: I don't mind. *(They embrace again)*
Naresh: Happy?
Leela: Happy. *(They break up. She sits down. He remains standing)*
Naresh: You don't mind the secrecy, the lies, the danger of scandal?
Leela: I don't mind.
Naresh: You don't mind that we can meet only once a week?
Leela: I don't mind. *(He goes down on his knees and puts his head on her lap.)*[3]

I would like to say two things by way of comment. First, that the dialogue here, though not particularly inspired, accurately captures the necessary secrecy of and the implicit tensions in such a liaison. More important, the stage-directions are sharp and clear. It is as if the dramatic element is never allowed to escape our attention.

Within the claustrophobic world of the marriage, these explicit directions assist in building up a tautened emotional balance which is perpetually in danger of being upset. And always, in the background, is the music, conceived of almost in terms of a pathetic fallacy, emotively echoing the action, occasionally swelling to drown all other sound.

It seems to be significant that Ezekiel's first major return to the dramatic mode in the '80s also handles the theme of domestic drama because in this later play *(Don't Call It Suicide)* the view of marriage is equally dismal and unredeemed. *Marriage-Poem* had one principal marriage—the visitors Ranjit and Malati are far too incidental. The second play explores several marital relationships set within the web of a single large family. Structurally, the play has two acts as against the single one of *Marriage-Poem* and each of these is in turn subdivided into scenes.

The earlier play had dealt with a failed marriage in unambiguous terms. The husband-wife dialogue, the dream-sequences where the wife's inner fears and the husband's involvement with another woman are dramatized, the perpetual wrangling, all emphasized the basic incompatibility of the two partners-in-marriage. There was no attempt to camouflage the failure of the relationship. *Don't Call It Suicide,* on the other hand, projects the sham security of a superficially placid, "working" marriage. In spite of a seeming harmony, it soon becomes apparent that there is little joy in this marriage either. Mr. and Mrs. Nanda are caught in a trap of conventional dependence on each other, but there is practically no genuine communion between them.

A single phrase sums up the ambience of the world the Nandas inhabit: middle-class respectability. The skeleton in the cupboard, a threat to this respectability, is that of their eldest son who had committed suicide some years earlier. The paranoia about even admitting that such a thing could have happened to them is expressed by Mrs. Nanda over and over again in a line that gives the play its title.

It is this paranoia that makes Mrs. Nanda resent her husband's visitor, Mr. Sathe. She suspects him of making Mr. Nanda maudlin, of reminding him of the event she would like him to forget. In a curious way the son's suicide and the secrecy in which it is shrouded remind us of the bizarre secret the couple share in *Who's Afraid of Virginia Woolf?*, though there is of course very little else by way of resemblance between the two plays. It might be worth mentioning here that Patrick Beck has compared *Marriage-Poem* to Albee's play, but it seems to me that Albee presents disturbing depths which *Marriage-Poem* lacks, perhaps because of its essentially Indian setting.

The setting is the most positive aspect, as drama, of both *Marriage-Poem* and *Don't Call It Suicide.* In the second play a composite picture of Indian marriage is variously presented. It is there in the mundane exchanges between Mr. and Mrs. Nanda. It takes a particularly virulent form in the characterization of the dead son's widow. A self-effacing, submissive girl, her non-status is sharply defined through the way others treat her. Mr. Nanda, essentially well-meaning, puts it in a nutshell by harping on her being "not even matriculate." By definition, therefore, she is uneducated, dependent and, to that extent, vulnerable. But it is Mrs. Nanda's response to this daughter-in-law and to the one not widowed but in some senses even worse off, beaten by her husband and coerced into giving up every shred of individuality.

Irony is implicit in the way Mr. Nanda and his son-in-law discuss cruelty on a large scale and seem impervious or blind to its presence in their own home in their treatment of the young widow.

Dramatically, the second play does not break any radically new ground. Like *Marriage-Poem*, it relies essentially on such obvious stage-devices as music, directions indicating the movement, position, and mannerisms of characters, etc. As in *Marriage-Poem*, the enactment of sequences both within and without the stage-action add a further dimension to the plane of reality.

Yet, though the later play is in some senses more "Indian," more typical if you like, I feel it loses out to the earlier one in the overall impression of homogeneity or even credibility. This is largely because the idiom in the first one is more sustained, uninflected, and does not distract through the use of obvious

Indianisms. In *Don't Call It Suicide,* such Indianisms obtrude into the dialogue, very often without any obvious justification. An example is I, i, quite early on in the action:

Nanda: We did our best to help him. He didn't appreciate it—never mind that. After he got his B.A., he told us he didn't want to go in for his M.A. We said alright, we are not tyrants. My second son and my daughter were doing very well in their exams. In fact, my second son got high second class in his B.A., and later my daughter got first class. Her marriage was arranged with a very successful business executive. Son also made a good match. Both are quite happy.

Mr. Nanda, as one has seen him so far, has not come across as a very strong individual perhaps, but his English has been nondescript and uninflected. His sudden lapses into Indian English don't seem borne out by the context. There are varying shades of Indian English and we all use them to a greater or less extent. But the kind of Indianisms Mr. Nanda periodically gives way to are not those that fit in with the way he speaks for the most part. The same is also true of other characters.

The problem of the right idiom is a major one, of course, and one that Indo-English dramatists and writers of fiction (perhaps more so than poets) must eventually face up to. I am not very sure how the problem can be solved, but I do know that unless a satisfactory solution is found this aspect of Indo-English writing will remain far from satisfactory. Perhaps a simple, unobtrusive style which conveys the mentality rather than aiming at accuracy in speech rhythms would be more suitable.

I must confess, finally, that I am not at all happy with the uneven roles Ezekiel allots his male and female characters. It seems hard to believe that the women are uniformly as drab, stereotyped and unimaginative as they are made out to be.

In *Marriage-Poem,* in spite of occasional indications that Naresh is partially responsible for the failure of the marriage, he comes across largely as a man who has made a disastrous marriage, the disaster of course being his wife Mala. The other women in the play are the self-righteous neighbour (Mrs. Lall), the gullible breathy romantic (Leela) and the flirtatious housewife (Malati). There is no ambiguity about the fact that Naresh is misunderstood and feels trapped, even crucified, within the marriage.

Similarly, in *Don't Call It Suicide*, the limited world-view is all Mrs. Nanda's even though her husband (recognizing his culpability as regards his son's death) himself commits suicide at the end of the play. Mrs. Nanda's daughter is the only woman with a degree of individuality, but her role is far too minor.

It may of course be argued that the playwright depicts Indian women the way they actually are. But, to be truly meaningful, such drama should eventually move beyond mere descriptive representation to inclusion of possible causes even if this is not done in too overt a manner. Such a commentary, even if oblique, would extend the range of dramatic theme and also strengthen characterization, both male and female.

NOTES

1. In an interview, *The Afternoon Despatch and Courier,* August 1, 1988, p. 9. The interviewer was Rochelle D'Souza.
2. *Ibid.*
3. *Marriage-Poem, Journal of South Asian Literature,* Vol. XI, Numbers 3-4, Spring, Summer 1976), pp. 165-66.

Theme of Alienation in Nissim Ezekiel's Plays

R. RAJ RAO

Nissim Ezekiel has not been as prolific a playwright as he is a poet. *Three Plays,* published by Writers Workshop in 1969, remains his only collection of plays in book form. Two one-acters, *Who Needs No Introduction* (described in the sub-title as "an unpoetic sketch, with embellishments") and *Song of Deprivation* ("a comic morality . . . for the non-existent underground theatre in India") have been circulating among friends and admirers in manuscript form. A sixth play, *The Wonders of Vivek,* has been recently completed and privately read to small groups of theatre lovers.

All Ezekiel's plays are seen to have a minimal build-up of action and sparse dramatic development, and this possibly explains why they are not usually staged in Bombay and other urban Indian Centres where a few professional theatre groups have come into their own. The intellectual content of the plays far surpasses their dramatic value, and the playwright seems to dwell more in the realm of ideas than in the sphere of histrionics. This, however, is not to undermine the merit of the plays or their intrinsic worth as literature. Ezekiel's plays may not abound in punch lines and witticisms calculated to draw peals of laughter. But they do reveal an artistic vision at once penetrating and ironic; and it is laughter of a subtler sort that they evoke, laughter at the larger comedy of life in which we are all players.

In the human comedy, the alienation of the individual from the social and cultural environment to which he belongs forms an important theme. If alienation be defined as "the action of estranging, or state of estrangement in feeling and affection" (as the

Oxford English Dictionary defines it), then the alienated individual is he who not only cannot relate to people and the surroundings, but who experiences a partial or total breakdown of communication, and leads a maladjusted and lonely life. Such an individual undoubtedly deserves our sympathy and the expert care of psychologists, but Ezekiel is more concerned with tracing the malady to its roots. Thus, while alienation is a unifying theme that runs through all his plays referred to above, it is possible to speak of types or categories of alienation that plague the lives of the playwright's dramatis personae.

Culture is a major factor that is responsible for an individual's isolation and loss of identity. Such things as race, habitat, dress, food, language and sensibility can hopelessly estrange people from one another. Whites are generally regarded as superior to blacks, browns and yellows, so in *Nalini* the fact that a white (an American) has told Nalini that he liked her paintings is enough for her (and Raj and Bharat) to believe they are worth an exhibition. What the credentials of this American are is a question that is never asked.

Natural habitat has much the same effect. Bharat's speech to Raj in the first act of *Nalini* easily explains why he says in act two: "I'm unreal. I am nobody. I am nothing . . . I'm an Indian, I'm not an Englishman." The relevant speech in the first act is as follows:

> Bharat: We are the busy, active men of the city. We are all in good jobs. Our houses are well furnished. We read good books—foreign books of course. We are not slaves of caste. We are not superstitious. We don't spit (He imitates a loud, clearing of the throat, and spits). We don't make loud, gurgling sounds when we drink our tea or soup. (He imitates the action, exaggerating). Our marriages are not arranged for us. We don't dream about dowries. We are not communalistic, provincial or parochial. I could go on like that for an hour. It is good that we are not what we are not. But what are we? Liberal, modern, advanced, progressive Indians? Are we Indians? And if we are not Indians, what are we?[1]

It is the city as a cultural unit distinct from the village that is here responsible for Bharat's predicament. In that sense a person may belong to the city and yet be a villager (in his attitudes). But if lifestyles in the city and the village are in such marked contrast to each other as to make upper-class urban men feel they are un-Indian, it is not surprising that Miss Ganguli in *The Sleepwalkers* has to write plays (much to the amusement of Mr. and Mrs. Morris) not for Indian audiences as a whole, but for village folk solely. Moreover, the fact that Mr. and Mrs. Morris are amused at this proves in itself that people from relatively homogeneous culture must never comprehend lands like India, where there is (to use that overtaxed phrase) unity in diversity.

Dress and language are important cultural emblems that can dissociate people from each other. This is superbly brought out in *The Sleepwalkers* in a brief scene:

> Mr. Morris: Have you been to the States?
> Mr. Kapur: Yes, I was there last year.
> Mrs. Morris: (To Mrs. Kapur) Did you accompany your husband, Mrs. Kapur?
> Mrs. Kapur: No, I couldn't go. At that time I was expecting.
> Mrs. Morris: Expecting?

Ezekiel, who has an ingenious ear for Indian English (his very Indian poems in Indian English are unmatched in flavour and wit), knows only too well that the awkward ing-construction ("expecting" in this case) is enough to alienate the (Indian) speaker from the (Western) listener.

In *Song of Deprivation* dress recurs as an instrument of alienation when, talking over the telephone, "She" becomes a "different woman altogether" as she takes off her bikini and gets into a sari. "He" at the other end describes her as "the social creature now . . . in the all-covering sari." "Social" here implies it is the only attire in which the woman can be accepted in the mainstream of Indian society; in the bikini she is ostracized, although as "He" tells her, in the sari it is "not the real you."[2]

Even the humourless disposition in the Indian psyche plays a destructive role. Hypersensitive Indians, overtly touchy, have no use for banter to which they can react but clumsily. In *The Sleepwalkers* the American publisher Mr. Morris almost seems to foresee this when he says ironically: "There is no humour in my magazine. When you laugh, you laugh *at* something, *at* somebody. . . . Individuals laughing at one another leads to nations laughing at one another, and ultimately to conflicts. Laughter is not necessary for peace of mind. He who does not laugh, neither shall he weep." By altogether avoiding humour in his magazine, Mr. Morris can doubtless be assured of a large readership in a country where people pride themselves on their seriousness.

The social alienation of the individual is yet another problem presented in Ezekiel's plays. In contemporary Indian society, the relation that one's trade or vocation bears to the social reality determines one's level of acceptance. In *Nalini* Bharat candidly admits to Raj that he has become a promoter of art because it is the only thing he can do well; he cannot gainfully do any other work. For example, he cannot uplift the masses or go to the villages. But how useful is Bharat's kind of work to suffering humanity? There may be "prestige in art, intellectual respectability and all that," just as it is "with theatre, dance, music, all the arts?" to use Bharat's own words. Yet Bharat fails to be one of those living on the soil of the earth. He belongs instead to an ivory tower of social prestige, a circumstance that is not exactly enviable for the aloofness it imposes. As compared to Bharat, the self-conscious speakers in *Who Needs No Introduction*, who includes the Chief Guest, the Chairman and the Secretary, are closer to the masses vocationally, but not by attitude. In effect, they are as preoccupied with their careers as Bharat is in *Nalini*. Sounds like the loud barking of dogs, the braying of an ass, the neighing of a horse, and a general din all around, skilfully woven into the texture of the play, indicate that the speakers are removed from reality: the audience cannot see them as their counterpart.

More pathetic is the plight of artists and "thinking men" doomed to a similar fate. The painter Nalini sees herself as being divided "into two persons." One, obviously, is the everyday Nalini, unimaginative but surrounded by friends. The other is the creative Nalini who "suffered from some unimaginable upheaval within her. She was alone, separated from humanity." The "first" Nalini described the condition of the "second" as one "of madness." Freud was right: the artist is insane. But talent seems to be bestowed on him as compensation not only for insanity but also for the hermitical state in which he finds himself. Naresh in *Marriage-Poem*, though no practising artist, is in an identical situation when he says:

> I am alone. It has taken me a long time to learn how to be alone. I've also learnt how to value the condition. The whole world is recreated when one achieves it. All art, poetry, music, everything that is true and beautiful is for the single man.

At the end of his speech Mala asks him: "What kind of language is this?" Ezekiel makes the point nicely: people may be able to respond to the work of an artist but can rarely understand the creative process; as a craftsman the artist is always alone.

The "thinking man," the man with a mind of his own, is different from the artist in degree rather than kind. He has the artist's intelligence but not his imagination. Socially, however, he is as much of a misfit as the artist. Hence, in "The Sleepwalkers" Mr. Morris argues, somewhat ironically, that thinking is the chief cause of division and unhappiness: "If we discourage thought, we shall decrease unhappiness. Modern technology has made it necessary for everybody in the world to live without thinking. Real living, the living that matters, is living by doing. The more we do the happier we are." In other words, man has to make the painful choice between intellectual alertness and inner tranquillity. Thinking as an activity may result in conviction. On the other hand, "When humanity doesn't think, it is peaceful. Thinking divides humanity into warring groups." To these words of Mr. Morris, Miss Ganguli adds: "This will be a very good thing for Bengal. People think too much there. That's why all this stone-throwing and burning of buses. If we had less thinking, we could have stable government." And a few moments later Mr. Morris clarifies: "Avoid thinking of anything in particular, even if you can't avoid thinking in general. Thinking in general does no harm. It's thinking in particular that's dangerous." It is this view that Fritz Blackwell[3] describes as "the anti-thought characteristic" of the play, which he feels is not merely present in the speeches quoted above, but is blatantly—but effectively—developed in the description of and references to the American magazine which the publisher wishes to issue in India." The happiest circumstance, then, is that of the archetypal Indian woman, the legendary mother, sister and wife, who enjoys complete social acceptance; she achieves this because, as Mr. Kapur says in the play, she gets along peacefully without thought.

On a third level, Ezekiel's plays suggest that there is something inherently offensive in our natures, in our very upbringing, that can upset the balance in human integration and culminate in alienation. The term "offensive" here needs to be interpreted in a strictly exclusive sense, implying that what is offensive to one man, one class, one race, one nation and one generation is not necessarily offensive to another. In *Song of Deprivation,* "She" on the telephone testifies this view. In a longish speech, she points out how she is alienated from her grandmother and other relations belonging to a bygone age, because their way of thinking, speaking and acting is repugnant to her:

> It's a kind of miracle, isn't it? I mean, how I escaped. All that suppression and repression. Half a dozen voices saying No to me from the time I was a child. No childishness permitted to me when I was a child. Don't do this, don't do that. You'll fall, you'll hurt yourself. No sympathy in adolescence. No freedom as a college student. Not allowed to read certain books. Not allowed to see certain films. Not encouraged to make friends outside the community. Where are you going? When will you be back? Don't be late. Suspicion and distrust from the beginning. Resentment of spontaneity. Hatred of everything modern. Fear of fashion. Awful. Imagine listening to

endless talk about money and property and food—yea, endless talk about food. The mutton today is very good. The mutton yesterday was not so good. It tastes better when it's hot, doesn't it, have some more, very special *masala* this, want a potato, take this chapati, it's got more ghee on it, this cabbage is excellent, I love cabbage—endlessly, endlessly. How I hate it. I always hated it. The atmosphere of gossip and petty-mindedness, the total indifference to ideas, the soulless routing of religious ceremonies without an iota of religious conviction, the muttering of long prayers without knowing their meaning, the hostility to everything new or different, without giving it a chance. Terrible. How can anyone live like that, as if inside a cage, how can they? It's absolutely sterile. They bring up *their* children exactly as they were brought up. They arrange marriages for them, and want *them* to bring up *their* children exactly as they were brought up. It's shameful! It's nauseating! How can such people ever relate anything. How can they understand anything. They're dead, dead, dead.[4]

In *Nalini* it is Bharat's pseudo-intellectualism and lack of genuineness that offend the lady. This is an important issue in the play; Anisur Rahman goes to the extent of saying that "The art-scene and intellectual pretensions of the central character are, in fact, the main focus of the drama while all other things are merely cliches designed to build an atmosphere for the play."[5] The fact is that Bharat promotes art and artists not because he understands them, but because it brings social prestige. Between art and artists, it is the latter, of course, that he understands better but again not with real psychological insight. As for art, Nalini correctly sums him up the moment he compares her paintings to Picasso's; it is this very moment that she probably decides not to seek his help for her exhibition.

In *Marriage-Poem* the husbands and wives are estranged from each other not only due to diverse levels of learning, but also because of confused value systems. This is clearly revealed in the following lines:

Mala: What are you talking about?
Malati: Dark paradoxes.
Mala: What paradoxes?
Malati: The paradox of vice and virtue resembling each other.
Ranjit: Nobody said that.
Mala: For me, vice is vice and virtue is virtue. There can't be any confusion between the two.
Naresh: In the space between the two, there is always confusion.
Mala: There shouldn't be.
Naresh: There isn't for you.
Mala: There shouldn't be, for anybody.
Malati: Everybody's not that simple.
Ranjit: I agree with Mala.

In *The Sleepwalkers* there is a classic instance of alienation by overstatement. Mr. Varma, the Hindi writer, unwittingly makes a spectacle of himself by reiterating to the American guest *ad nauseam* that he has written "one hundred and eighty-seven short stories" and "four hundred and seventeen poems" and by undignified pleading with him to use his "great influence" to have his stories printed in the American magazine.

Similarly the Chief Guest in *Who Needs No Introduction* fails to realize how ludicrous his speech sounds to his listeners. The giggle of a young woman in the audience, twice distinctly heard as the Chief Guest is ranting, proves that the offensive something in our natures can at times be so powerful as to repel *our* people, let alone outsiders.

As an un-didactic creative writer, Ezekiel is content to present the problem without (by and large) offering solutions. However, in one play—*Nalini*—there is a hint at a desirable course of action. Ironically enough, the words are spoken by Bharat himself:

I don't know clearly, but I know there is another way. It would

> require us to care more for our talents, to take care of them better, to be more involved in the world around us, to commit ourselves to something more than our comforts and pleasures.

It is also of interest to note that while he diagnoses the malady, Ezekiel would like us to take a sympathetic view of his characters. In *Nalini* Bharat is made to say: "But I'm a man. I'm a human being. I've got feelings. I've got needs. . . . I think and I *am,* yes I *am.* I don't know what I *am,* but I am. You can't wipe me out. You can't cancel me out." Further, we are made aware that intellectuals like Nalini have to cope with an identity crisis throughout their lives. Nalini asks Bharat:

> How long can I keep this other woman at a distance? Her experience is necessary to me. Without it I am nothing. I can never become an artist.

Bharat himself has a double vision of Nalini—a dream Nalini and the real one.

In like fashion, "He" refers to two "Shes" in *Song of Deprivation*—the real one in the bikini, and the social one in the sari. She, then, must certainly suffer from an identity crisis. And in *Who Needs No Introduction,* the three speechifiers are convincingly portrayed as types estranged not merely from their audience, but also from each other.

It may be said, by way of conclusion, that Nissim Ezekiel shows a keen psychological perception of human nature and captures, in his plays, the strife of human interaction more effectively than most Indo-English dramatists. After a reading or a performance of his plays, one is likely to view life less self-consciously, and grasp the significance of empathy. In fact, many of his characters seem to be especially designed to heighten awareness. It would be fairly reasonable to say, for instance, that the trio in *Nalini,* the couples in *Marriage-Poem* and *Song of Deprivation*, the Indian and American guests in *The Sleepwalkers* and the speakers in *Who Needs No Introduction* typify men and women with like propensities, who are telling us through their stories why we fail. None of these characters is fully developed in the psychological sense; or to put it differently, none of these characters is round. Yet Ezekiel shows considerable psychological prowess in understanding them as types. For it is not the playwright's intention to trace the growth and individual development of specific persons by delving deep into their psyche, as much as it is to study overall communication patterns of representative human beings transacting in a complex world, where contact, in the widest sense of the term, is both a necessity and a difficulty.

NOTES

1. Nissim Ezekiel, *Three Plays* (Calcutta: Writers Workshop, 1969).
2. "Song of Deprivation" (MS).
3. Fritz Blackwell, "Four Plays of Nissim Ezekiel," *Journal of South Asian Literature,* Vol. XI, Nos. 3-4 (Spring, Summer 1976), p. 270.
4. "Song of Deprivation " (MS), 11.
5. Anisur Rahman, "Technique and Motif in Nissim Ezekiel's *Three Plays,*" in *Indian Writing in English,* ed. Krishna Nandan Sinha (New Delhi: Heritage, 1979).

Panel Discussion on Gieve Patel's *Mister Behram*

Transcribed by Toni Patel from recorded documentation of the session. The panel discussion, chaired by Ms. Priya Adarkar, took place on January 31, 1989, at the Department of English, University of Poona, a day after the performance of the play at the Tilak Smarak Mandir, Pune. The participants included the playwright, the director of the play, academics, intellectuals and students. The discussion provided a unique opportunity for direct communication and feedback between the creative artists and a critical audience.

R. Raj Rao: I would like to comment on certain aspects of the play: homosexuality, for one. Apart from that, the question of language. The play is set in the nineteenth century and the language is formal, classical—even in the intimate scenes between Naval and Rati or Naval and Behram, the idiom is formal. If the play were set in the twentieth century, would the playwright try out a different idiom, something more colloquial, informal, or would it be the same. I'd also like to refer to the servant boy. Now in the servant boy who doesn't speak a single word we see Naval as he must have been when he first entered the house. Naval too entered the house as a servant boy and there are references to that and Rati in fact asks him jokingly whether he would like to come back to the kitchen and even he speaks about it. So that is an important role and I would like to ask both Gieve and Toni how they arranged the servant boy's exits and entrances, as I feel they were quite meaningful.

Neela Karnik: We were talking about the theme of the play and I thought that there was the theme of power and colonization that occurs at two levels: in the land and also the boy. Behram takes on the onus of trying to reform this boy and create him into a kind of a model. The boy is always an enigma at the heart of the matter. We have only Behram's word for the fact that Naval changes his mind so often; we don't hear Naval doing that at all. He is in fact very quiet, mute and reticent. My second comment is upon the production itself. One found a sense of poetry and mysticism operating within the play, yet the presentation of the play is realistic. Now, was that deliberately done for the audience? I found a problem as to how to correlate one kind of level at which the play was operating and the fact that everything was presented realistically.

Adil Jussawalla: I am glad Dr. Raj Rao brought up the problem of homosexuality and narcissism and, in fact, reminded me of a problem I have with the play, perhaps the only problem, which is the disintegration of Mr Behram—it appears to be very sudden. I have a problem with the play's time-frame. I am not entirely aware as to how long it takes for the action to take place so that when Dr Rao points to Mr Behram's poise in the beginning and the sudden collapse of it is, at least for me, difficult to accept an almost overnight transformation—though of course, it is not overnight. So how long does it take for him to get to that state? However, I do not find the poise in the beginning unconvincing. I mean, Naval is ultimately the object of his passion, but in the beginning of the history of the relationship he is the adopted son and he is also a son-in-law and Gieve has very subtly indicated that this problem is not just homosexuality. It is incest and I think a person in that kind of position would be hovering at a certain level as indeed Naval himself does. There is the time when Naval says something about being enveloped in a cloud and that he is happy to be in that state. It is the first time he is made aware of his own feelings, of Mr. Behram's feelings for him and he is on the point when he is going to submit. So I think at a certain point of the play Mr Behram takes a decision: "to hell with it, I know what's happening and I'm going to surrender to this passion." I think this is a play about a man surrendering to his own narcissism and lack of self-knowledge, if you like, and therefore destroying himself. But I agree I don't know exactly what the turning point is. There was a particularly objectionable comment made in a review of this play that appeared in a Bombay newspaper. The gist of the argument was such: "well, we all know what's going on right from the beginning. It's only these fools on the stage who don't know." This is an objectionable viewpoint because that is the very point of drama. We know what's happening to Desdemona. Like the lady who shouts from the audience at Othello: "You fool! can't you see what's happening about the handkerchief?" Surely that's the point of drama and I'd like the playwright and the director to comment on that particular criticism, if they feel it is worth commenting on at all.

Prashant Sinha: I have several points regarding the themes of this play. I shall comment first of all on the factors and the psychological problems. I think you can also find a distinct element of sadism and masochism. There is no doubt that Naval is a masochist—he enjoys the pain that is inflicted on him. Mr Behram is a sadist in relation not only to his son-in-law, but also to his wife. I think his sadism is quite as manifest as the masochism of Naval when we know that there is something very inadequate about the relationship of Naval to his wife. It is in no way a fulfilling or a really consummated erotic relationship. There is something inadequate, something lacking in the relationship. We can also perhaps talk at length about the Telemachus theme in the play, the entire complex of the father-son relationship.

Then, coming to the presentation of the play, I thought there was a great deal of self-dramatization among the characters and I can see that justified in the case of Mr Behram. I think Behram constantly dramatizes himself. I did feel though, that certain other characters's dramatizing themselves or playing their own roles was perhaps—and I have read the play only once—was not entirely and fully justifiable. I do want to refer briefly then to the beginning of the play. It is effective because in certain ways the early gestures and actions are embodied in what the play contains and as we know good plays do have a scene towards the beginning or towards the end that is a mini-play containing the entire action of the play. As we know generally in drama a convulsion or a fit stands for the denial of personality. I am thinking at the moment of Osborne's *Luther* where the famous fit very clearly embodies the denial of Luther's monkish self. We could say that Naval's fit is symbolic of his denial of his present personality. Let us also not forget that the dream contains a goat. In the western tradition certainly the goat embodies sexuality and I think we could trace that link—let us not forget that Parsis are among the most westernized of the communities in India, so I guess we can't overrule the western tradition—in fact, that tradition is inherent in the play. Then coming briefly to certain aspects of form. The format is, as Neela said, naturalistic, though some of the dialogues are highly poetic. In fact, in more ways than one, the drama text reminded me of Ibsen, for example, the focus on two or three characters at a time. One didn't find much ensemble acting, because the other naturalistic mode—the Chekhovian mode—involves a large number of characters on the stage. You (addressed to Gieve) worked on the basis of two or three characters and tried to portray relationships in rich and considerable depth and in poetic language. You seem to have followed the unity of place and, possibly, of time. I thought that the music used was slightly unusual. We would have preferred either strings or something that is more soothing or conventional. Well, these are most of the remarks that I have to make.

Adil Jussawalla: There is just one thing that strikes me. I am a little troubled about the parallel of the goat (laughs) and westernization. Take the symbol of the owl, for instance. Westerners do not regard it as a symbol of ill-luck as we do. It is an interesting point you've brought up—but I'd like to ask the playwright.

Toni Patel: (interrupting) Adil, you've just said the owl is a bad or ill omen in the Indian tradition, but it is also regarded as such in the West. Shakespeare mentions the sound of the owl as an ill omen.

Adil Jussawalla: Yes, but to call someone an "ullu" means to call him a fool, and in the West, the owl stands for wisdom. So it's all very complicated, depending on which strand we pick up, so I'd like to ask the playwright. Perhaps there is something in the Warli tradition with which you are very familiar.

Gieve Patel: Frankly, I've got a very pragmatic answer to this. I happened to see a kind goat being born in an identical situation, the kind of thing Naval describes. One evening, coming out of my grandfather's house in Dahanu district, I saw this happening and I said to myself that somewhere or other at some time in my life I would use this bloody thing! (Laughter, in which the audience joins). And in fact the first—as soon as I started writing this play—in fact, even before the characters had clearly developed and the trend of the play had been worked out, I remember that one of the first things that I had in mind was that I could begin the play with this image. So I put it in and in fact several times during the subsequent writing of the play over the next two years I was very uncomfortable with it and wondered whether I was imposing something that does not really belong to the play. And then I thought that I would trick my way through and make it work anyway.

Ashok Kelkar: I find something disturbing about Dr Rao's and Professor Sinha's comments. I think that they are reductionist. This is a baffling play. Naturally, bafflement is not a very pleasant state particularly for a critic because he has to explain things and that is where I think the motive for reduction comes in. This is "masochism," this is "narcissism" and this is only "homosexuality" and so on. There are two things to note as starting points. Two important insights of twentieth-century criticism as I see it are the following: The creativity of an artist is as much a matter of intelligence as it is a matter of the imagination. What strikes me about the play is how intelligence and imagination are both active in the play. To take intelligence at a very elementary level, look at the very cunning of the construction of the play—you are carried along with it. The play begins in a relaxed manner—there is a degree of uncertainty; there is a fair amount of comedy in the initial scenes: social comedy and so on—and then suddenly, you find yourself in deep waters and drawn into the current, as it were. At the same time, there is this element of imagination. It is not easy to capture both Warli and Parsi. In one sense, the play is very local. This position of South Gujarat and Thane district is a kind of continuous ecological tract in which several tribes, including the Warlis, live. Parsis own big holdings in that area. Some of you may recall the Warli revolt led by Godavari Parulekor. Warlis are remarkable in various ways. I know of them partly because two of my students did field work in that area on the Warli dialect. One of the problems that they had was that the Warlis are very taciturn. A linguist usually prefers to be among talkative people, because then he can get lots of data but here he had to really work hard to get them to speak. So they tried the other strategy, used by linguists to gather data—namely, of merely sitting quietly in a corner while listening to the Warlis talking among themselves but found that this does not work either. Some of them were also working on a neighbouring dialect and they had no problem there at all—so the usual kind of reticence that a tribal may show towards a city person was not the sole explanation. In fact, some of the other tribal people commented on the fact that the Warlis don't talk. Apparently, their entire expressive genius is revealed in the pictures they draw. Warli art is justly famous, and one or two Warli artists have made a name. Now, despite not having any first-hand acquaintance with Warlis, I do feel that the author has imaginatively entered into the Warli consciousness, although he may not have detailed acquaintance with the Warli myths the way a folklorist could. He captures the Warli consciousness at two points: in the beginning and then later when Naval is passing through a very critical stage of whether or not to accept Behram's command to wear the Warli outfit and the transformation this brings about. At one point, Naval significantly says that his job as a lawyer is meaningless, as he should really resume his life in his tribal context.

So the play really moves at various levels. The other critical insight I had in mind was that of the old dichotomy between a formalist approach and the approach that concentrates on the content and meaning of the play. The moral and political dimensions of the play cannot be separated either. They are thoroughly integrated with the form of the play. That is where I find this reductionist approach most disturbing, because it tends to abstract these ideas and relate them to ideas of philosophers or theoreticians like Freud who present theories which try to explain human life. The basic motivation of an artist is not to explain human life but to understand it. If at the end of the play, we find that we have a dim idea of what it is to be a Nahnu-Naval, this would probably be a slightly more fruitful way of getting into the play, and thus, making valid comments about it. Only after this process of internalization can we afford to comment on the play.

Prashant Sinha: May I mention that the comments made by Raj, Neela and myself are complementary. I didn't say that the play had only this problem.

Ashok Kelkar: My comment was that your remarks were reductionist in the sense that something or other is nothing but a, b, c which can fit into some psychological or sociological framework . . .

R. Raj Rao: One didn't say "nothing but" . . .

Ashok Kelkar: No you didn't say that.

Neela Karnik: I think you are right about an integrated approach. You do however descend to reductionism whether you like it or not, in critically assessing the play. What exactly do you mean by getting into a play.

Ashok Kelkar: One way of getting into the play is to take out the various moral and political strands in the play—the way power is exercised at various levels: colonial power, the power to the landlord and of one man over another—and also the moral strand: the old Kantian problem of to what extent one man can be the means to the end of another man. Now the days when people could be shocked by talking about homosexuality are over. The problem, in assessing a homosexual relationship, is whether the partners are in love with each other. Love implies that you accept the other person as a person, and not as a means to one's pleasure or as a pawn in one's power-game. What is, then, Behram's "original sin?" It is not homosexuality. At this point, it might be useful to compare the play with other works of art. I was thinking of *The Tempest* but there are, of course, obvious differences, but in a sense Naval is a combination of Caliban and Ferdinand. Then, of course, there is this other theme: the position of women. Another important strand in the play, complementary of the main theme, is of whether one human being can entirely be looked upon as a means to another human being. I think in one sense, that is one of the things that the play is about.

Prashant Sinha: Dr Kelkar, you haven't said anything about form. You said that you were going to tell us about form. So far you have talked only about meaning.

Ashok Kelkar: Yesterday, when I talked about the form of the play, I said two things. One, the play proceeds through moves, unlike a novel that proceeds through episodes. Two, that a play lets you enter from the front door of the present and work your way into the future. Now if you use these two strands, I think a number of the formal features of the play could be set out in great detail.

Aditya Agnihotri: At the outset, I would like to congratulate both the writer and the producer for a very well-contrived script and an equally well-contrived presentation. With regard to the theme, it may seem local, but I think it has universal appeal too. Mr Behram is a man fighting against himself and against the norms of society, in instigating social reform. Mr Behram confronts this inner conflict day in and day out. He puts on a brave front against social criticism and yet suffers his own doubts and inner conflicts. Mr Behram's hypocrisy lies in becoming lyrical over every trite subject. Behram's lyrical admiration of Naval-Nahnu is at odds with the humiliation to which he subjects Nahnu; this outrages the feelings of Dolly and the audience.

I think the success of the production lies in the fact that one is sucked into the play and swept along with it. However, I do think that the use of sensitive mikes could help avoid presenting Mr Behram's outbursts as rhetoric or ranting. An effective device would be for Mr Behram to project his inner conflict through his facial expression, while a tape recorded voice—over emerged from the wings, I think that would add to the intensity.

Ashok Kelkar: Incidentally, the inner conflict also comes out in the way he switches back and forth between calling him Nahnu or Naval.

Vrinda Nabar: I am not so sure about whether this device of using electronic media and facial expressions would really work. I don't know whether you've seen Olivier's *Hamlet*, but you are put off at the very beginning, with the first soliloquy when Laurence Olivier very melodramatically throws his head this way and that and the voice in the background says: "Oh that this too too solid flesh. . . ." It is very unsuccessful.

Toni Patel: However, I think that it is a very interesting possibility; the only thing is that it is not the way in which we conceived this play. It is possible to have another production where one could use the device you suggested and it would work very well, I feel.

Dnyaneshwar Nadkarni: Please, please don't do that, because it is a very dated device and Marathi productions are full of it. (Laughter) Even the best intentioned plays still use it. It is a terrible, horrible device.

Toni Patel: Mr Nadkarni, it is always a question of how you use a device.

Dnyaneshwar Nadkarni: No, no, no. I am very stubborn on this point.

Adil Jussawalla: May I just interrupt? Would like to comment on Mrs Karnik's observation? I think she made a distinction between the language of the play and the way it was produced.

Toni Patel: Actually the production is naturalistic and not realistic—it is poetic lyrical naturalism and is within a particular convention.

Neela Karnik: You know for instance you had the music, then you have the boy's entrance and exits that Raj was talking about operating in the play.

Toni Patel: The music is simply a convention. In this case, music, as always, is a problem. Any lyrical music poses such problems because, as it is, there is music in the language and I didn't want anything to interfere with that. So finally, we used Warli music simply as a means, a signal to the audience to indicate the beginning and end of each act, so that it did not interfere with anything else.

R. Raj Rao: But how would that justify the stand that the production is poetic?

Toni Patel: I am not justifying that. I leave that to others. I'm only saying what my attempt was, and I'd like to say something else. I very much liked what Professor Kelkar said about reductionism being limiting. My attempt, all through, has been to take the play as a whole. When discussing a play—let's take *Macbeth*—people will always argue what it is about—there are always many interpretations in the productions which take only one aspect and push that. In this case, I tried not to do that, to take the whole thing, every aspect of it.

A Student: I wish to comment further on the music. I find that there is a deliberate disharmony between the audio part of the play and the spectacle. By audio, I mean the music, which I found very significant because it was tribal. The music is used between acts and evokes the tribal ethos which is not actually depicted in the spectacle, except in the instance when Naval is made to wear Warli garments and once when Naval speaks about his childhood and wishes to return to his tribal life. Except for these two instances, there is no other indication of the tribal music. Hence, the deliberate use of tribal music, used very sparingly of course, very intelligently, actually indicates the tribal background against which the elitist drama takes place. So the tension between the tribal situation on the one hand and the elitist on the other is very interesting.

Priya Adarkar: I think that applies to very similar things (Laughter). Would Pushpa Bhave comment?

Pushpa Bhave: To begin with, about the topic we were discussing.

I felt the music is very important in this sense, that to begin with the playwright didn't succumb to the temptation of having the Warlis seen actually on the stage; also the music denoted the emotional patterns, I felt. The violent emotions around the small round table twice in the play, which are denoted by drum music, had a semiotic significance for me. The drawing room scene—though as Toni pointed out, it was not a drawing room drama—really depicted Behram's cultural milieu, and in contrast his inner conflict came out really well, though it was subdued, so I liked the music and the way in which the director maintained the tension. The Behram-Naval relationship is a very complex one—to me, it embodies the idea of *possession*—in many senses. A relationship of the conqueror and the vanquished. Earlier, the Parsi background of the play was mentioned. I have seen Gieve Patel's *Princes* and feel that that play was intended to portray the decadence of the Parsi Dahanu milieu. In *Mister Behram* I feel that the situation is far more complex: Behram resists subservience to the British, on the one hand, and yet tries to possess Nahnu. . . .

Adil Jussawalla: To continue that idea, I think that the character of Mr Watts, the District Collector, takes the play right out of the confines of a lot of contemporary drama. I think it is a very important step for an Indian playwright to make because it is also a comment on Empire.

Ashok Kelkar: I feel that the transformation of Mr Watts from the ineffectual man in the beginning of the play to the scheming one at the end of the play reminded me of Shakespeare's history plays. The transformation of Prince Hal to Henry V, for instance. The point is that all of these side themes add up to the main theme: the psycho-political dimensions of the relationships between human beings.

Another point I would like to consider. . . . You talked of the naturalistic style that you adopted. I think that the naturalistic style was useful in the following manner: it allows itself to be used as a neutral base, a transparent glass—just like the drone, the tanpura in the background in Indian classical music—so that all the other matters could be played against it. As for the pseudo-lyricism, it could be seen to be pseudo only against such a naturalistic background. Had the presentation been more poetic, perhaps the pseudo-lyricism would have passed off as genuine lyricism. Then, of course, there are truly poetic moments and poetic flourishes in the language—and then the language itself—and occasionally the music—are allowed to carry the burden. This points to the fact that the playwright is deliberately keeping certain things neutral. To digress a little. . . . Let us compare Shakespeare to Racine, there is an immediate difference. For example, with Shakespeare the language is rich and loaded with imagery, whereas with Racine, one gets a very bare kind of language. Linguists tell us that while Shakespeare's vocabulary is voluminous, Racine's is very limited. Racine also uses the drawing room French manner, a very courtly and civilized way, despite portraying elemental passions. I think that the naturalistic acting is complementary to the extremely civilized modality in which these characters interact with each other. The characters are forever sorting things out and, of course, finally the sorting out comes to a literal dead-end. There can't be any further sorting out and then the vision that you get at the end of the sorting is not bearable.

Toni Patel: Actually, Racine was very much on my mind when I was directing the play, and I think it is very much on your mind, Gieve?

Gieve Patel: Racine is always on my mind. (Laughter) Right through, from the very first play. I may move away in every other direction, but I always come back to him. I mean that in a certain kind of way, to me, in the representation of pure human passions, no playwright comes anywhere near Racine. He is just the distillation of human passion.

Priya Adarkar: . . . in the mind . . .

Gieve Patel: . . . very much in the heart as well.

Prashant Sinha: In Racine we generally get a blend of honour and passion.

Gieve Patel: It is only in Berenice that you have honour and passion as a theme. Phaedra doesn't care for her honour two hoots.

Prashant Sinha: I mean that she is aware that she is doing what she should not be doing, and the passion is so powerful.

Gieve Patel: I find it difficult to verbalize but in some very instinctual and deep sense, wherever I read a Racine play, I feel as if I have been given a phial with a fluid in it which is pure passion.

P. Udayakumar: I just want to make a couple of comments on one of the points which Dr Kelkar raised. It is about the question of language which comes up in the play. I think it probably provides a kind of mediation between some of the thematic strands we have been considering and questions of form, because one of the problems which I had with the play yesterday, was that I found it too wordy, to begin with and then I have been trying to question myself and find out how this wordiness actually functions in the play and contributes to the peculiar disturbance which we find towards the end of the play. So in that sense, I think there is the theme of articulation—a kind of excessive articulation in the beginning and towards the end, culminating in silence—particularly in the case of Mr Behram. And I think that it is related to two other things which Neela Karnik and Raj Rao brought up. One was the question of love and possession and the other, the question of power. The law courts in a sense function as a kind of metaphor for this excessive articulation in its relation to power; towards the end

Behram's disintegration naturally has to culminate in silence, in an inability to speak because the foundation of this excessive articulation is a lack of a recognition of the other. Some of the themes like narcissism, incest and other psychological categories can be contextualized in this light. It is not enough to say that Behram's problem was narcissism or that his problem was homosexuality and there is this metaphor of an excessive articulation and interpretation of another person until you reduce him or her to transparency. That comes up in the metaphor of stripping. When you take off clothes, you are trying to reduce a person to transparency, only to discover that the body is something sensual, which cannot be articulated in words.

Ashok Kelkar: It's the theme which comes in Gieve's poetry.

P. Udayakumar: That's right. So I found that the theme of jealousy and theme of possessiveness like in Proust, for example, functions in this context of excessive interpretation and an attempt to reduce someone to transparency, and there are certain things which are counterpointed against this. Of course the vision of Naval in the beginning of the play and the black goat and what it symbolizes operate on a different level of linguistic perception than the law courts in the way of articulation. You can never reduce the black goat to this or that, which is so interesting. Similarly, the tribal music also probably functions as a reminder, as a counterpoint to what this language of the law courts excludes. Therefore, I feel that all the points raised earlier, about psychology and colonization seem to converge in the issue of articulation and that explains to me a little bit of why the play was wordy. The play had to be wordy to end in silence. That certainly relates to the remarks Dr Kelkar made about the naturalistic setting against which this wordiness can stand up.

Ashok Kelkar: The crux of the matter is I think the mood and the moves which add up to the play, which may be musical, in the form of gestures and movements, like stripping the boy, and at the same time, there are verbal moves, as well. Behram is both liberal to and possessive of Naval. On the one hand he wants the Warli boy to find himself, and so gives him all encouragement and, on the other hand, his homosexual passion is simply again a metaphor for this basic human refusal to let other human beings be themselves—a craving for power and possession.

P. Udayakumar: Yes, I agree with you that the moves can be verbal, though it wasn't clear to me in the beginning about the relevance of the verbal moves. I think that the homosexual passion of it has something irreducible about it, in relation to the question of gender. As for the question of articulation given to women, Dolly is jeered at towards the end because the two main characters had to be silent and the articulation was given to the women characters. So I think if we try to question ourselves about moralistic judgements, about the naturalness or unnaturalness of homosexual passion, I guess we would be asking a slightly lopsided and probably misguided question. I think the question of homosexual passion here certainly needs to be seen in the light of the representation of gender.

Ashok Kelkar: The males form an exclusive club from which the women are kept out.

Prashant Sinha: It is a system of exclusion that operates here, whether it is manifested in narcissism or colonization. This probably makes possible the problem of articulation.

Ashok Kelkar: It is also significant that those cultures that have exalted homosexuality emphasize the exclusive male club—I mean West Asian and the Classical Greek cultures. In India, where a maternal culture operates, homosexuality has always been looked down upon as one of those weaknesses that one has to live with, but certainly without admiration. While homosexuality comes up in Socratic dialogues, for example, in a good deal of classical Persian poetry, you do not find such representation of it in Indian art.

To return to the Parsis, as Dnyaneshwar Nadkarni pointed out, Parsis have been a figure of fun, to other communities. I think Parsis themselves to some extent contribute to this in the sense that at least publicly, they don't take themselves seriously. The stock cliché in films and theatre is of the mad Parsi. Maharashtrian observers of the Parsis always find them intriguing and, of course, it is typical to laugh at what you can't make sense of. There are various dimensions to the enigma of the Parsis. One is the ambivalent status of the Parsis in Indian society. On the one hand, they have identified themselves with India—look at the role of the Parsis in our freedom movement, for instance, or in the Indian classical arts of music and dance. Yet, Parsis have also identified themselves with the colonizers—in excelling in Western classical music—people like Zubin Mehta—and the fact that Parsis send their children to English medium schools and affect to know English better than the English. At the same time, they have not abandoned Gujarati. So this tension is always present. In setting the play in the late nineteenth century, Gieve Patel has chosen the time when this ambivalence was full blown. Today's Parsis are a different picture—all sorts of other complications have entered.

The play is both very local and very universal. I agree with you about the universal elements of the play—these have not merely to do with self-justification; there are various other universal elements like what I call the whole power business. But these universal elements are realized very locally so they come home to us as realities that we can recognize.

Aditya Agnihotri: Could I just add a point to the issue of the "wordy play." I consider it as part of the theme of communication. I find excellence of the play in the speeches. The verbal strategies used and the nuances picked up and deliberately left out certainly are of a sophisticated nature. Naval picks up the thread of Behram's argument sometimes and, occasionally, deliberately ignores it. As far as interpretation strategies go, there is a difference in the intention and the final outcome of an act. In the party scene, the two set against each other. This mixing is very subtle, refined and poetic.

Sunil Ganu: To pick up on the structural importance of the party scene, I wonder if any of the panel members would like to comment on the "sati" and at what level it acts. Simplistic and reductionist as it may sound, I saw the "sati" as a foreshadowing of the removal of Behram at the end. If you believe in the power game that Neela Karnik spoke about, indeed Nahnu has been very clever in playing this power game, attentively agreeing and disagreeing with him. I thought that the mention of the "sati" was a way of foreshadowing what was to come.

Prashant Sinha: May I request Gieve Patel to talk briefly about psychology.

Gieve Patel: If I may quickly put forward one point that Raj Rao has brought out, because I am interested in the observation as a writer. Raj Rao pointed out that in the whole script there is very little instruction about the servant boy. I know there is one point where Behram tells him to go and bring the Warli costumes and then asks him to get tea. But Toni has taken the servant boy and made something else out of him—I'd like Toni to talk about it.

Toni Patel: What I would like to say is that it is not of my own making. It just happened that it was necessary that the Warli should be there as a silent counterpoint. However, as you know, many of a director's decisions are based on practicality—it works out from there and then something I suddenly discovered as leading somewhere. First, I just needed a Warli to pick up plates and take them out and clear the stage and so on, and I used that in the Japanese convention of using a person who is not part of the action. In Japanese theatre, you have a man who is dressed in black clothes who just comes in and goes out and is not part of the action at all. But when I had this man there—this silent man coming and going, I suddenly realized he is important and the very silence of this man acted. What Professor Kelkar mentioned about the silence of the Warlis seemed to help—to establish the counterpoint—so we used it. I then consciously used it as a device. I also talked a lot to the actor who plays the Warli servant about the psychological background, his reaction to the action and to the other characters. All that has been worked in through the silence—the audience is not entirely conscious of what's going on, but he is there—very much a part of the action. It is one of those things that just happened and yet had to be. I can't conceive of this production without that silent person. Besides, the silent Warli is also a motif in Gieve's plays. In the last play, *Savaksa* too, we had a silent Warli. Again we discovered in that play that he was very important.

Dnyaneshwar Nadkarni: While discussing the production, I would like to point out something. Though there is a uniformity of good acting and a good production, one must be careful over certain details. When the tea is poured, nobody knows how to pour it—the speed and rhythm of pouring from a kettle are just not quite right. Although I know that there is no tea, that action betrays quite a lot.

Priya Adarkar: I think we need to return to the question that was asked about psychology.

Prashant Sinha: I was told that you do have an interest in psychoanalysis.

Gieve Patel: Well, psychoanalysis has been very important to me since the age of nineteen. I have undergone an extensive psychoanalysis myself for severe problems that I had at that age. I don't think I would have survived without it. And then of course, after twenty years of an acquaintance with it, I could take it over into my own hands and it has become an almost lifelong instrument with which to watch one's own mind—and then other disciplines also begin to enter in. As you grow older, you discover that the techniques offered to you by one therapeutic form are echoed by other psychic and intellectual disciplines as well. I want to say that psychoanalysis is so important to my life as to permeate all my activity.

Toni Patel: But you wouldn't say that your play is Freudian?

Gieve Patel: Oh, no ! Let me say that when I take on any extra-artistic discipline in order to understand myself and the world. I am very careful to see that its intrusion into art is very measured, because what I loathe is artistic expression which spouts the id, the ego and commonplace Jungian images. In the same way, if one were to enter the study of mysticism and absorb it into one's life, one would have to be very cautious as an artist not to prattle on about the kundalini.

Dnyaneshwar Nadkarni: In connection with this background in psychoanalysis, where do you find it in your painting?

Gieve Patel: It is not apparent in any of my work. It is all under the surface.

A Student: Why did you make the play so intense? After the interval it just went on and on.

A Voice: That's your problem.

Toni Patel: We just wanted you to suffer very much!

Gieve Patel: Masochism!

Priya Adarkar: Thank you very much. Thank you.

Contributors

Aditya Agnihotri	Academic, Lucknow
Chandrashekhar Barve	Academic (retd.), Pune
Arun A. Bhagat	Academic, Pune
Pushpa Bhave	Academic, Bombay
Veena Noble Dass	Academic, Hyderabad
Vrinda Nabar	Academic, Bombay
Dnyaneshwar Nadkarni	Theatre critic, Bombay
Toni Patel	Theatre director, Bombay
R. Raj Rao	Academic, Pune
P. Ramamoorthi	Academic, Madurai
Shubhangi S. Raykar	Academic, Pune